"I was already recommending this book before I finished reading it, for Arthur Paul Boers is an outstanding (yet humble) mentor, guiding our steps into the Way and ways of Jesus. He recounts his pilgrimage warmheartedly and at a trekker's pace so that we are gently invited to enter into it and engage in its lessons. If you walk with him on the ancient path he treads, you will find yourself inspired, questioned, disturbed and transformed."

MARVA DAWN, author of *The Sense of the Call* and *Keeping the Sabbath Wholly*

"In a postmodern world in which time and space seem compressed and lives of leisure are driven by frenetic consumption, we should not be surprised that many have turned to the medieval practice of pilgrimage as a vital spiritual antidote. Arthur Boers's reflections from his pilgrimage on the Camino de Santiago stand out for their honesty and gentle wisdom. As a Mennonite participating in a medieval Catholic spiritual discipline, Boers fills *The Way Is Made by Walking* with startling insights and fresh perspectives into the spiritual journey that all must make."

RICHARD R. GAILLARDETZ, Murray/Bacik Professor of Catholic Studies, University of Toledo, and author of *By What Authority?*

"Pack your fantasy knapsack; walk with Arthur Boers on the adventure of a lifetime, the five-hundred-mile pilgrimage to Santiago de Compostela in Spain. What a lively, sensitive, down-to-earth and deeply spiritual guide Boers is! His tales as a pilgrim will so captivate your imagination that you could find yourself in real time, walking stick in hand, making your way along that sacred path made holy by the faith of countless pilgrims."

KEITH J. EGAN, Saint Mary's College/Notre Dame University

"Everything seems up for grabs, and nothing seems fulfilling any longer. But in this unassuming and engaging chronicle Arthur Boers shows that gravity and grace can be recovered step by step. And for those of us who can't go on a pilgrimage, there are wonderful lessons to be learned from one who did."

ALBERT BORGMANN, author of *Real American Ethics*

formatio
TRADITION. EXPERIENCE.
TRANSFORMATION.

Formatio books from InterVarsity Press follow the rich tradition of the church in the journey of spiritual formation. These books are not merely about being informed, but about being transformed by Christ and conformed to his image. Formatio stands in InterVarsity Press's evangelical publishing tradition by integrating God's Word with spiritual practice and by prompting readers to move from inward change to outward witness. InterVarsity Press uses the chambered nautilus for Formatio, a symbol of spiritual formation because of its continual spiral journey outward as it moves from its center. We believe that each of us is made with a deep desire to be in God's presence. Formatio books help us to fulfill our deepest desires and to become our true selves in light of God's grace.

THE WAY
IS MADE BY
WALKING

A Pilgrimage Along the Camino de Santiago

Arthur Paul Boers

FOREWORD BY Eugene H. Peterson

IVP Books

An imprint of InterVarsity Press
Downers Grove, Illinois

InterVarsity Press
P.O. Box 1400, Downers Grove, IL 60515-1426
World Wide Web: www.ivpress.com
Email: email@ivpress.com

©2007 by Arthur Paul Boers

InterVarsity Press® is the book-publishing division of InterVarsity Christian Fellowship/USA®, a movement of students and faculty active on campus at hundreds of universities, colleges and schools of nursing in the United States of America, and a member movement of the International Fellowship of Evangelical Students. For information about local and regional activities, write Public Relations Dept., InterVarsity Christian Fellowship/USA, 6400 Schroeder Rd., P.O. Box 7895, Madison, WI 53707-7895, or visit the IVCF website at <www.intervarsity.org>.

Scripture quotations, unless otherwise noted, are from the New Revised Standard Version of the Bible, copyright 1989 by the Division of Christian Education of the National Council of Churches of Christ in the USA. Used by permission. All rights reserved.

Scripture quotations marked "BCP" are from the Book of Common Prayer.

"Bless the Lord" on p. 176 is taken from Songs and Prayers from Taizé, and is reprinted with permission of GIA Publications.

Excerpts from "Little Gidding" in Four Quartets, copyright 1942 by T. S. Eliot and renewed 1970 by Esme Valerie Eliot, reprinted by permission of Harcourt, Inc.

All photographs were taken by the author and are used by permission.

Design: Cindy Kiple
Images: border: Li Kim Goh/iStockphoto
*   hiker: Timothy Epp/Dreamstime.com*
*   map: Piers Nicholson/the Picture Pages at www.santiago-compostela.net*

ISBN 978-0-8308-3507-2

Printed in the United States of America ∞

Library of Congress Cataloging-in-Publication Data

Boers, Arthur P. (Arthur Paul), 1957-
   The way is made by walking: a pilgrimage along the Camino de
   Santiago/Arthur Paul Boers.
     p. cm.
   Includes bibliographical refereneces.
   ISBN-13: 978-0-8308-3507-2 (pbk.: alk. paper)
   1. Boers, Arthur P. (Arthur Paul), 1957- 2. Spiritual biography. 3.
Christian pilgrims and pilgrimages—Spain. 4. Spain—Description
and travel. I. Title.
   BR1725.B594A3 2007
   263'.0424611—dc22
                            2007021558

P   21   20   19   18   17   16   15   14   13   12   11   10   9   8
Y   26   25   24   23   22   21   20   19   18   17   16

"A true friend sticks closer than one's nearest kin."

PROVERBS 18:24

This book is dedicated to fellow pilgrims
who were companions to our family
from both sides of recent transitions
and who have become kin to us:
Alan and Eleanor Kreider
John Oudyk and Sandra Mooibroek
Becky and Tom Yoder Neufeld

CONTENTS

FOREWORD

—

There is nothing more pedestrian (literally!) than walking on a way, a
road, a path. But the moment we put one foot in front of the other, we
very well might find ourselves on a pilgrimage. Walking could turn out
to be the most significant spiritual act in which we will ever engage.
And the road we walk on the holiest piece of ground. Feet and faith
are inextricably integrated. This book is a witness, extravagantly docu-
mented and compellingly narrated, of how feet and faith dance together in a life well lived.

Arthur Paul Boers writes the story. One summer he walked five
hundred miles, as he says, "to go to church." The church was the cathedral in Santiago, a pilgrimage destination, on the northwest corner of Spain. The road he walked was the *Camino de Santiago*, on which
millions have walked over the last twelve hundred years. It took him
thirty-one days.

Pilgrimage is the ancient practice of walking, usually with others, to
a holy site while paying prayerful attention to everything that takes
place within and without, soul and body, all the ways that are inherent
in the Way, along with the companions who are also on the Way. It is
not as simple as it sounds. It is not the spiritual equivalent of taking a
holiday walking tour through Scotland, say, or walking across America
supporting the cause of cancer research.

Before reading this book I knew that pilgrimages to the Holy Land and Rome and Canterbury had long been a part of our Christian tradition. And I knew that visiting holy sites by airplane, train and bus was still a popular tourist activity. But *walking* five hundred miles?

I had no idea until I read Arthur Boers that millions of men and women all over the world are still doing it, deliberately paying attention to what takes place in and around them as they walk to their chosen destination. He narrates his conversations with those with whom he walked, Christians and non-Christians. He teases out details that interlace in the intricate complexity of what he experienced in this intense juxtaposition of feet and faith.

Way is the most prominent metaphor both within and outside Scripture for enlisting our imaginations, and hopefully our involvement, in living concretely, responsively, immediately, with our muscles and bones, brains and voices, the nerve endings in our fingers and the calluses on our feet on the actual dirt, carpet, asphalt or concrete that is under our feet at any given moment: all the ways that are implicit in walking on any way, road or path that we happen to be on. Destination is important—essential. But the way we get there, walking over mountain passes, across deserts, through heavy rain and scorching sun, is where the action takes place. And the ways we experience the time and terrain, companionship and conversations as we walk.

Boers doesn't so much tell us *about* pilgrimage as invite us, in his lively and colorful prose, to join him. We get to see and get a feel for just how it works, the ways the way pulls all of life—blisters and body odors and fatigue, winsome conversations and spontaneous hospitality—and maybe most of all prayer into a comprehensive life. We are immersed in a compelling documentation—detail after detail, conversation after conversation—that prayer on the road has to do as much with feet as with faith, moving, in his words "at the speed of life."

As we accompany this pilgrim on the Camino de Santiago for these thirty-one days, Jesus' well-known metaphor, I am the Way, has a chance of making its way into our ways, permeating all the parts of our lives. This is a book to savor and read and then reread as we learn to *live* pilgrimage so that we will never again reduce walking to just getting across the street.

Eugene H. Peterson
Professor Emeritus of Spiritual Theology
Regent College, Vancouver, B.C.

ACKNOWLEDGMENTS

—

Therefore, since we are surrounded by so great a cloud of witnesses,
let us also lay aside every weight and the sin that clings so closely,
and let us run with perseverance the race that is set before us,
looking to Jesus the pioneer and perfecter of our faith.

HEBREWS 12:1-2

Walking the Camino de Santiago was the most intense experience of solitude in my life, but I did not do it alone. I am deeply indebted.

Many pilgrims from around the world heartened me on the journey: Brother Paul and Brother Domingo, Jean-Louis and François, Claude and Willem, Felix and Nichole, Helena and Pilar, Olaf and Annette, Xabi and Juan, Mike and Araceli, Markus and Susanne, Ton and Joke, Curtis and David, Hisako and Theresa, Chandon and Mary, Otis and Felipe, Cindy and Wendy, Jan and Angela, Aileen and Elisabeth, Carole and Ursula, Jeff and Eileen, Simon and Jane, Violant and Mercedes, Agnes and Uta, Rosa and Feliz, Hendrika and Stefano. Most of these folks I will never see again in this life, but I wish them all a hearty and grateful *¡Buen Camino!*

Our church small group helped me dream about this pilgrimage, blessed us the night before departure, patiently suffered through my many photos afterward, and even read drafts of this manuscript: Ray and Aki Epp, Twilla Epp, Ray and Sonja Gyori-Helmuth, Andrew and Katie Kreider, Colin and Lora Rusel, and Marcia Vierck.

Associated Mennonite Biblical Seminary is a rich setting to live out my vocation. Several colleagues showed particular support for this venture: Barb and James Nelson Gingerich, Alan and Eleanor Kreider, Nelson Kraybill, John Rempel and Mary Schertz.

A belated word of appreciation to Viola and Paul Fretz; they understand why.

Two organizations crucial to my pilgrimage and my hiking are the Little Company of Pilgrims Canada and the Bruce Trail Association.

The Louisville Institute and William Brosend graciously supported two writers' retreats: Writing as Pastoral and Spiritual Practice, at Cathedral College, and the Writers' Asylum, at Collegeville Institute. Those occasions tremendously advanced this endeavor. Thanks as well to fellow writers at both events and especially the directors of those occasions, Dean McDonald and Don Ottenhoff, and our instructors as well, Nora Gallagher and Cindy Malone.

I am grateful for the honor of working with InterVarsity Press and especially with Senior Editor Cynthia Bunch.

I also appreciate the work of Melissa Fisher Fast and Samuel Voth Schrag as research assistants for this project and the contributors to the appendix on pilgrimage locations: Alissa Bender, Erin Boers, Roy Hange, James Junhke, J. Nelson Kraybill, Alan Kreider, Eleanor Kreider, Marlene Kropf, Willard Roth, Ray Simpson, Glenn Edward Witmer.

I am particularly grateful for the support and love of my family, our children Erin and Paul, and my wife Lorna McDougall. Lorna generously supported me on this venture. In the fiftieth year of her life and right around our silver wedding anniversary, she also accompanied me for the first part of the journey. By the time she departed, I knew I wanted to get home as soon as possible!

God steadily leads me into life along a *buen camino*—and always does so with good company indeed.

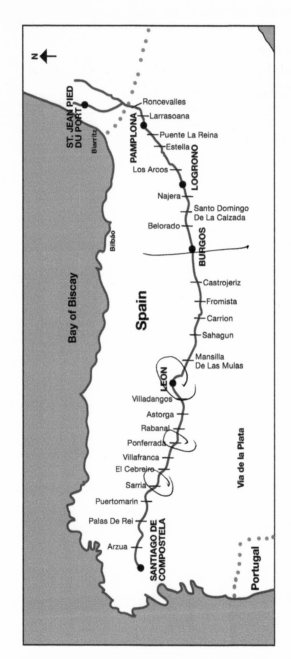

The Camino Frances Pilgrimage Route. Most cities on the map are a day's walk one to the next.

INTRODUCTION

—

For I am but a sojourner with you,
a wayfarer, as all my forebears were.

PSALM 39:14 BCP

TAKE THE LONG WAY

I once walked five hundred miles to attend church. It took thirty-one
days, but was no month of Sundays. I usually go by foot or bike to our
local congregation, but being on the road this long for a worship service—in a foreign language, no less—was an unusual stretch even for me.

To be more accurate, I was on a particular pilgrimage route in
northwest Spain, the Camino de Santiago. (*Camino* is Spanish for
"way" or "path" and *Santiago* simply means "Saint James.") Its destination is the city of Santiago de Compostela. There, a cathedral houses
the purported relics of James the apostle, patron saint of Spain. This
was one of three main pilgrimage destinations for medieval Europeans
(competing with Rome and Jerusalem). Millions walked there in the
last twelve hundred years, and it has grown popular once again.

I was not only going to a church service, of course. People often say
that pilgrimage is more about the journey than the destination itself. I
had many reasons for this trip: meeting pilgrims, seeing a new country

from ground level, reflecting on church history, practicing a classic spiritual discipline, developing my appreciation for walking, and challenging myself physically. Yet I could exclude any one of those motives and still call the trip a pilgrimage. But without finally getting to Santiago at the end of the route, visiting the Cathedral and attending the service there, the traveling—while exceedingly worthwhile—would not have had the same focus and direction. It would not have been a pilgrimage.

So, in a sense, I did walk five hundred miles just to go to church.

Pilgrimage Paradoxes

In some ways, I still have trouble believing that I was even interested in this pilgrimage, let alone actually walking it. Five years earlier I was on another trip to Europe. I traveled to communities of prayer in several different countries. I considered that venture a pilgrimage and as a result studied Christian pilgrimage traditions. I kept encountering the importance of medieval Santiago, which was new to me, and also discovered that this route was experiencing renewal. I was not at all interested in it and could not conceive why anyone would have attempted it then or now. How quickly people change!

There were, I know and confess, many ironies and paradoxes on this Camino.

It was somewhat absurd to travel in vehicles thousands of miles roundtrip just to walk five hundred miles. (My return journey involved a bus, taxi, train, minivan and no less than five jets.) For someone who professes concern about minimizing our ecological footprint, perhaps I should have traipsed closer to home. Why not just step out of the house and begin? Well, for one thing, not every walk is a pilgrimage. And more than that, alas, I cannot think of any noteworthy long-distance walkers' routes near where I live, let alone paths and tracks worn into the earth and made hallowed by centuries of passing pilgrims.

This big, spacious country has little hospitable room for walkers and even less in the way of holy sites. Many settle instead for gas-consuming pseudo-pilgrimages to megamalls, Las Vegas, sports stadiums, Star Trek conventions, Graceland (second only to the White House in visitors!) and Disney World. Seventy million people a year go to Orlando, Florida.

There was a time when pilgrimage meant traveling far, usually by walking, from *wherever* one happened to live. Continental Europeans went to Santiago from the doorstep of their homes, whether in Belgium, Germany or Austria, traveling for months. Now, tens of thousands of Santiago pilgrims annually move by plane, bus, train or car to some more convenient place to begin by foot, bike or even horseback. (I did meet a few hardy folks who had walked all the way from deep in France, the Netherlands or Switzerland.)

While a five-hundred-mile pilgrimage may sound pious—and I admit to some self-righteous pride about this—it was a tremendous privilege. How many people can afford such a prolonged excursion? More than once someone asked, "What do you do for a living that makes this possible?" As a seminary professor, my school-year schedule freed me up.

But here is another wonder: How is it that people of our day, with the longest lifespans in history and a glut of "labor-saving" devices, find it astonishing to think of committing serious time to a spiritual endeavor? Cees Nooteboom marvels about medieval people who "set aside their lives to walk halfway across Europe in dangerous times." They knew they might never return. Their lives were short, but they risked them anyway. Commenting on the Islamic commitment of going to Mecca, Nooteboom noted that Muslims now use contemporary modes of transportation—much as Santiago pilgrims currently do. For modern Muslims and Christians alike, "the longer they live the less time they have." Surely people of our era with all our labor-saving devices could afford *more time* for matters of the spirit.

There were other paradoxes. When the local paper did a generous story about my journey, several folks contacted me in disbelieving perplexity at why I did such a strange thing. They found it odd that this Protestant—a Mennonite, no less!—went on pilgrimage, a seemingly Catholic practice. Reformers roundly renounced pilgrimages, especially the connection to indulgences and the adulation of patron saints.

And while I greatly admire the apostle James, I was not comfortable with how he has been used by Spanish nationalism. I appreciate notions of James the *Peregrino* (pilgrim), but feel deeply disturbed by James the *Matamoros* (Moor killer). Spain's patron saint became the figurehead for Christians wresting control of this country back from Muslim Moors, and he later served as a mascot for the Crusades as well. In many churches along the Camino, and in the Santiago Cathedral itself, I saw images of James angrily waving a sword and riding a charging horse that crushed beneath him various hapless victims.

As it happens, James was himself a victim of state-sponsored violence (see Acts 12:1-2). In fact, he was the first apostle to be murdered, the first of Jesus' companions and inner circle of disciples to be slain. Yet here, in Spain, he was usurped to justify violence. That would be like naming nuclear weapons after the Reverend Martin Luther King Jr., the famous Christian advocate and practitioner of peacemaking. As a Mennonite, convinced that faithfulness to Jesus clearly requires nonviolence, I loathed what I saw. My distress was deepened by a current reality: in the twenty-first century, Christians justifying bloodshed against Muslims is again disturbingly common. Jesus' rebuke to James and his brother John, who eagerly wanted to punish inhospitable Samaritans, still speaks sharply to us: "You do not know what spirit you are of, for the Son of Man has not come to destroy the lives of human beings but to save them" (Luke 9:56).

A prominent paradox of my sojourn—and the one that surprised and taught me the most—is the fact that so few fellow pilgrims I met counted themselves as Christians. How curious that many immersed themselves in a taxing route associated with church traditions for over a millennium but did not necessarily profess Christian faith. And these folks ended up teaching me more than I realized I needed to know. (Stories and examples in this book are based on real people and events, but some names and details were altered to protect the privacy of individuals involved.)

While this Camino was an expression of my Christian faith, what I did was not especially noteworthy or sacrificial. I encountered hundreds of people along the way. Tens of thousands now walk it every year. Many—perhaps even a majority—go without an explicit religious agenda. I met extraordinary Christians on those paths, but also remarkable, gracious and hospitable people of no declared faith. Do we Christians think too highly of ourselves? Are we perhaps on the same journey as everyone else? Often people who most challenged me with their exemplary way of living, both on this path and elsewhere in my life, were folks who did not call themselves believers.

In spite of all these contradictions and conundrums, questions and unresolved uncertainties, I had a deep sense of being called by God to that pilgrimage. A longing that was hard to name drove me to undertake something that I could not have imagined even a few years ago.

VERY HARD AND INCREDIBLY GOOD

This journey was one of my most satisfying life achievements ever. When I returned home, people asked how it was (followed by predictable inquiries: "How are your feet?" "How long did it take?"). I summed up the journey by saying: "It was very hard and incredibly good." As I read and reread my trip's journal, I seldom see any day that was simply easy. And sometimes more than one day felt like the hardest so far! Some stretches of the path were so intense, demanding and challenging that I needed all my concentration just to put one foot in front of the other, and I dearly hoped no one would try and strike up a conversation. But every day also had unforeseen blessings and compensations. I learned much in that month and suspect it will take me years to unpack and integrate it all.

As I walked, I was never sure whether I would write a book about the experience. I'd heard a disparaging remark about the number of prospective authors on that particular route and felt self-conscious about that. I did keep a journal. Yet my journaling did not necessarily reflect any intention to write in detail later; I have been a journaler for decades. When companions learned I was an author, they teased me about my intentions. Even when I got home, I still had not decided whether what I'd experienced merited a book. But, without any explicit plans, I began writing every day after I returned. I could not let it go, or perhaps I could not be released by the Camino. Gradually, a manuscript emerged.

There have been other comparable periods in my life. When my father and mother-in-law died relatively young only six weeks apart, I kept rehearsing those events and their meaning for a long time. After a bitter church conflict, it took a painstakingly slow year of counseling, prayer and licking my wounds before I could learn from that and finally let it go. In each of these instances—let's face it, traumas—I encountered challenges that changed and transformed me. I did not welcome those opportunities; I endured them. I had no choice about experiencing them, only in what I would do with those experiences. They all reworked me. Long after the trip was done, I kept pondering it. I set my computer to use Camino photos for desktop pictures and screen savers. Even without such aids, the pilgrimage was always on my mind. Over a year later I still recalled vignettes and incidents every day. Each night, when I lay down, I revisited scenes. When sleep was long in coming, I would recall every place I stayed along the way. As I went for walks, uninvited memories flooded my mind. I always wanted to tell stories about my trip to others, whether visiting friends, sharing a meal with my family or teaching classes. I worried that I might become a bore. I could not stop thinking about what had happened. It took only a month to walk but required much longer to process.

Walking the Camino was not a trauma, although it is the most demanding thing I have ever done. The pilgrimage differs from those sorrowful circumstances of loss and grief because I chose it. And apart from my perpetual drivenness to complete whatever I begin and the possibility of losing face, I could have cut it short and gone home whenever I wanted. But I did not. While not emotionally traumatic like those griefs, sorrows and tragedies experienced during my life, the pilgrimage also reworked me. I could not stop thinking about it because there was too much to take in at the time of the walking. And, more than that, it was calling me to change my way of living. Pilgrimage "unites belief with action, thinking with doing" and requires that "the body and its actions express the desires and beliefs of the soul." Pilgrimage is about integration, body and soul, feet and faith.

On the Camino I was drawn into an ancient spiritual practice, pilgrimage itself. I prayed much and considered what it means to follow Jesus. I expanded my understanding of spirituality and heard God's call to simplify my life. I read once-familiar Bible passages as if for the first time. I confronted truths about myself and my own compulsions, matters that I might rather avoid. And I caught glimpses of hospitality and collaboration that I knew would reorient how I live my daily life. I felt challenged by God to pay closer and more respectful attention to spiritual seekers who see things very differently than I. And I grew more enamored with the spiritual gift of walking. I was deepened in discipleship.

Like many Christian pilgrims before me, I experienced major themes of our faith on the way: providence, penitence, evangelism and faithfulness. I learned to trust God's provision, even in adversity. I grew in self-awareness, reviewed my life, recognized major blocks in my Christian walk and recommitted myself to spiritual growth. I spoke with many people about Jesus. And I pondered faithful ways to live in our consumer and materialist culture. The pilgrimage has implications for all my life, and that is why it takes me so long to keep processing it. Thus I still mull it over. The work is not done. As one fellow pilgrim, Stefano from Italy, wrote me after the journey: "The Camino works in me . . . step by step."

PILGRIM'S PROCESS

Two Protestant classics, John Bunyan's *Pilgrim's Progress* and C. S. Lewis's *Pilgrim's Regress*, reflect earlier eras where spiritual growth and formation had clear stages; advance or decline was almost measurable. But we live at a time when our walk with God is seen as more fluid, including steps forward and backward, perhaps even sideways at times, and we are not always sure which is which. Indeed "journey" is such an important metaphor in our culture that it is now a virtual cliché; we're all on a journey it seems.

My pilgrimage yielded many unanticipated results. I knew I wanted to begin in St. Jean-Pied-de-Port, France, and end in Santiago de Compostela, Spain, and was aware of some physical geography along the way, but was unsure about how or even whether I would experience God. I had plans and some straightforward goals; I had an approximate itinerary. But none of this was any assurance that this would be a pilgrimage. I was uncertain what, if anything, God might say to me along the path. This journey was a *process* because it challenged and re-worked me in ways I could never predict.

Change the accent and *process* is a verb with spiritual connotations. In religious ceremonies, celebrants and participants move in a common direction as part of their worship, minipilgrimages. Such rites are pow-erful. Many in my generation and faith tradition are suspicious of re-ligious rituals and routines. But often the most hardened anticeremony persons are moved when they walk in—or even observe!—a wedding or funeral procession. Something in our hearts is not touched by in-tellectual assent alone. Our feet and bodies need to join the action. The Camino is a processional of thousands.

THE WAY IS MADE BY WALKING

Catherine of Siena used to say that "all the way to heaven is heaven," reminding us that in the spiritual life ends and means are bound up with one another, and a sojourner's progress really is about one's pro-cess. In fact, that powerful quote is of even more relevance to pilgrims when we hear the rest of the sentence: "because he said, I am the Way." When we journey with Jesus, all our lives are caught up in the process of his redemption and transformation of us.

Jesus not only called himself "the Way," he was often underway as well. A good part of his life, already as a child in Mary's womb, was spent en route. And the bulk of his ministry and teaching was on the road. Being faithful to God's Son always resembles journeying.

The title of this book is derived from a line in a poem by early-twentieth-century Spanish poet Antonio Machado: "*se hace camino al an-dar*" or "the way is made by walking." These well-known words have taken on a life of their own, as we can see by Googling them. I reflect on this phrase in terms of Christ the Way and my desire to know him better. Jesus calls us to live out and practice what he taught and modeled, to walk his walk. On the Christian journey we grow and learn best by practicing what Jesus preached. All pilgrimage—whether one day, one month or an entire lifetime—unfolds before as God leads and we are invited to follow. The Way commended by Christ has to be journeyed; it is made by walking.

> Show me your *ways*, O LORD,
>   and teach me your *paths*. (Ps 25:3 BCP, emphasis added)

One summer, this middle-aged man set out on the classic pilgrimage route of the Camino de Santiago, walking thirty-one days to travel five hundred miles. I climbed mountains and wandered through valleys. I sauntered in sunshine and trudged in drenching rain. I moved through old, abandoned villages that looked like ghost towns and through big and busy bustling cities whose noise overwhelmed me after hours of rural solitude. Sometimes the path was dirt or compacted mud, sometimes paved. At times I trekked over ancient cobbled and rutted Roman roads or smooth sandy tracks. Through it all, God led me on the way to life.

I

—

I WANT TO BE IN THAT NUMBER

Drawn to Pilgrimage

—

Therefore lift your drooping hands and strengthen your weak knees,
and make straight paths for your feet,
so that what is lame may not be put out of joint,
but rather be healed.

HEBREWS 12:12-13

NO PLACE I WOULD RATHER BE?

"What have I done?" I asked myself in panicked despair. It was the lowest point of my pilgrimage so far and the day was soon going to get worse yet.

It had taken all my wherewithal to trudge a quarter mile from the hospital emergency room to this park bench, and I did not know how I could go any farther. My left foot throbbed painfully from the bagel-sized blood blister that the ER nurse had just drained and tended. Every step ached, even though both my feet were elaborately swathed in white bandages.

Having arrived in the city of Burgos, I had been underway for two weeks and walked about 180 miles of my pilgrimage so far. I was in a particularly pretty part of town, near a cosmopolitan university. A shallow river glided slowly under arched stone bridges. Mature, fully leaved trees on a wide boulevard leaned over the riverbanks, reflecting the vibrancy of summer. But I was hurting too much to savor scenery and I was fretting about whether I would have to cut my trip short.

People of all ages strolled by, looking a lot healthier and happier than I. I watched them and longed for company, but they ignored me. I had just phoned home to my wife, Lorna, in the United States a few minutes before, and she had given me good words of consolation and encouragement, but now I was by myself again. On the sidewalk I had tried hailing taxis—by calling, gesturing and whistling—but each one whizzed by.

For the moment I could go no farther. I hung my head in my hands, feeling sorry for myself, wishing someone would help me, but knowing that I was on my own in a distant country.

But here's the thing: there was no place I'd rather be. I fiercely missed home and especially Lorna. Still, I was not yet ready to cut short my pilgrimage.

My biggest fear in the emergency room was that the nurse would order me to stop walking the Camino. Happily, she did not. Even so, disconsolately sitting there on that bench, not even sure how I could get myself to the hostel, I wondered whether I would be able to continue on the pilgrimage. It was the worst moment of my trip so far.

And yet I dreaded the thought that the journey might be over.

MOUNTING CASUALTIES

As time wore on, the physical toll had begun to show, and not just on me.

In a large city hostel (also known as *refugio* or *albergue*) in Logroño about a week into walking, I felt so tired that I could not understand how I would be able to move the next day. Most mornings were a resurrection when I surprisingly could travel, a dead man walking once again. A number of us in the hostel moved around barefooted, savoring the cool ceramic floors that soothed our overworked and overcooked feet.

I had plodded slowly that day, favoring a foot with a nasty blister that I actually felt explode en route. This wound eventually evolved into the one that landed me in the Burgos ER. It may have been my imagination or even just my projection, but in the Logroño shelter it looked to me as if more and more people were hobbling.

Within the first week of the pilgrimage, we began hearing about fellow pilgrims who were forced to take time off or leave, either because of accidents or general wear and tear. These could be interrelated. Injuries often were a result of tiredness. One physical problem might lead to others. Favoring a leg because of blisters or aching muscles could cause greater strain on the other leg. If a pack created hip sores and you radically shifted how you carried it, that might adversely affect your shoulders or neck. And so on. Some had to rest as long as a week to ten days because of the seriousness of their problems. Tendonitis was a common affliction. People diagnosed each others' ailments and freely offered medical advice.

As we discussed others' injuries and physical problems, we did so with deep concern. We were all sad when a companion could not complete the pilgrimage. It was easy to empathize with folks who were unable to continue. We could imagine how hard that might be. And as this outlandish endeavor was not a competition, we did want others to succeed. On my first day I encountered a woman who was trying to walk in spite of serious physical ailments. All along the route, I held her up in prayer, even as I was not sure that she could do this. Imagine my delighted surprise when I met her again in Santiago at the end of the journey, after not seeing her for four weeks.

But I confess that not all my feelings were pure and charitable. I knew that those aborted journeys could be mine—and indeed I came close with serious blisters first on my left foot and tendonitis later in my right leg days before arriving in Santiago. And while I cared for those who were forced to stop, I did not "want to be in their number." I longed to be one of the saints who marched into Santiago de Compostela. What compelled me to embrace this old Christian practice of pilgrimage?

DECIDING TO FOLLOW JESUS

James the apostle, *Santiago*, was a major inspiration—dare I call him a "patron saint"?—of my sojourn. A vital prayer discipline for me on this route was to lead, reflect on and pray with Scripture texts that mention him. He was one of Jesus' twelve disciples, brother of John, son of Zebedee, one of the "Sons of Thunder." There are surprisingly few entries about him, even though he was part of Jesus' inner circle, along with his brother John (the beloved) and Simon Peter. James manages to be present at many key moments in Jesus' ministry. Still, it is a largely silent life. Seldom does he say or do anything by himself, except in the manner of his death.

Yet the sketchy outlines of his life deeply challenge me. Not only does he leave family and occupation (because of God's call, not for career advancement), he hits the road with Jesus, takes many risks, often gets things wrong, and regularly merits correcting by the Lord. His understanding of power, violence and self-righteousness need constant challenging; his priorities require examination. Finally he gives up his life and dies a martyr.

The first New Testament passage about him is in Matthew 4, an account repeated in other Gospels. Jesus calls brothers James and John, and they leave their nets—and their father!—immediately. (Their mother shows up in subsequent stories, so she followed Jesus at some point as well.) They began a journey, a pilgrimage of sorts, full of uncertainties and unlooked-for hardships. What they anticipated and hoped for was often wide of Jesus' mark. James and John get corrected more than once. Reading the honest record of their fumbles helps me take heart in the face of my own persistent short-comings.

As I embarked on this journey, I wanted to testify to this vision of James, one grounded in the Scriptures. This Camino pilgrim path still challenges the status quo and converts people, as I witnessed again and again. I repeatedly caught compelling glimpses of God's reign, one that trumps hierarchy and divisions, competition and greed, violence and disdain. All of these themes echo and resonate with lessons James learned in his own unfolding pursuit of Jesus the Way.

I have tried to follow Jesus all my life, although I never responded to the call as dramatically or with the same risks as that son of Zebedee. In a small way the pilgrimage was a crucible for living out and examining my Christian life and faith to this point. It was a time of prayer and reorientation, the most profound spiritual retreat of my life. God challenged me in some ways familiar and others new.

SAINTS AS SIGNPOSTS

In early Christian history, ordinary church people were inspired by the faithfulness of notable Christians and began venerating relics (remains) of saints, honoring places where these notables lived and ministered. Thus began the tradition of pilgrimages to shrines. Margaret Visser notes, "Sainthood is perhaps the only honor accorded a person without consideration of physical beauty or prowess, wealth, birth, political power, intelligence, fame, or talent; a saint is admired, and considered exemplary, entirely for being good." Saints are to be signs of Jesus; they point us toward Christ.

Santiago de Compostela was one such saint-oriented shrine, the third most important pilgrimage center in medieval Europe. Legend had it that James evangelized in that region soon after Pentecost and that his body was miraculously transported there after his martyrdom. In the eleventh and twelfth centuries alone hundreds of thousands— if not millions—of pilgrims went there. James is one of only a few apostles honored with a tomb. (Peter's and Paul's remains are said to be in Rome.)

The other major medieval pilgrimage centers were Rome and Palestine. (See appendix three for information on Rome and Israel as current pilgrimage sites.) Rome was a center of political and ecclesiastical power. Palestine was biblically and geopolitically significant. Santiago de Compostela, on the other hand, being geographically and politically peripheral, was primarily important as a shrine. Most went there on pilgrimage, not for other kinds of agenda.

Sojourning to Palestine is most familiar to us. Some claim that *saunter* comes from the French, *Saint Terre* or "Holy Land," a reference to pilgrimages to Palestine. (Or so Thoreau asserted; he was not too shabby when it came to walking, often doing so four hours a day.) I like to think that walking makes any place holy.

Alas, a justification for the violent Crusades was to retain access to and possession of the so-called Holy Land. To this day, people contend—often violently—for control of such sites. As Palestine grew more dangerous and inaccessible in medieval times, European shrines such as Santiago gained prominence.

Pilgrimages were demanding and costly, even deadly, because of wild animals, accidents, bad weather, illness or violence. Pilgrims endured hunger and great physical exertion. A group of twenty religious sojourners going to Palestine in the twelfth century lost over half of their members to exhaustion. Even if pilgrims managed to return home, their long absence may have meant decreased opportunities for success, affluence or promotions. There were countercultural costs and implications.

My Burgos blisters and later struggles with tendonitis were obviously nothing in comparison. Still I was caught off-guard. Only recently had people come to expect travel to be restful and leisurely. Prior journeying was risky, hard, uncertain, expensive and taxing. In fact *travel* is closely related to *travail*, which means suffering. (In French, it means work.) Touring for pleasure and relaxation did not begin until the nineteenth century, when the concept of "tourist" emerged. It carried the notion of ease and enjoyment without exertion. Scott Russell Sanders says we "stripped the holiness from travel with our commuting, our tourism, our idle shuttling about."

This was the hardest journey of my life, certainly not casual tourism, but I'm glad that I did it. And the travail of that travel bore fruit. Whenever I felt sorry about this self-chosen hardship, I remembered faithful people who had no choice about their journeys. I recalled stories of refugees forced to walk far greater distances on hard roads in strange places. And doing so possibly with scanty food, fearing for their lives and without the benefits of sturdy footwear, rain gear and well-placed hostels. Perhaps in a small way this journey could teach me something about solidarity with such folks. It reminded me that a life of faith is not a rose-petal-strewn pathway. Faithfulness is no guarantee of everything going swimmingly. But it does powerfully link us to Jesus the Way and the costly courage of his final journey to Jerusalem.

By embarking on the Camino, I was stepping back—literally so—into an old Christian practice. I knew that walking the way of James could teach me a great deal about the true Way, Jesus the Christ.

TRAVELING MERCIES

That day in Burgos got worse. I finally managed to drag myself slowly back to the hostel. I reported to the manager that the nurse had ordered me to take at least one day off. When I requested that I might rest and stay a second night, he curtly ordered me to return to the hospital to get a document from the nurse explaining this necessity. I resisted the temptation to ask whether he'd like a note from my mother as well. My heavily bandaged feet moved him not at all. I could not imagine walking all the way back to the hospital in my condition. Too angry, frustrated and tired to think, let alone argue, I complained to a few acquaintances before going for a two-hour nap. And then matters gradually began improving.

After resting, I felt somewhat renewed, especially when I learned that the manager had changed his mind. My acquaintances had intervened and persuaded him accordingly. Even better, I discovered that two friends from Arizona that I had met earlier on the trip, Chandon and Mary, were visiting the hostel. They were eager to hear my story. I was no longer alone.

That evening, as they prepared to go out for supper, they offered to bring back some food so I could rest. But I needed company more than anything else. Outgoing folks, they gathered a circle of half a dozen or so people and off we went, Mary and I limping all the way and smirking ruefully at how absurd we hobblers looked. Chandon graciously invited me to join them and another companion, Theresa, from Canada, for a few days. Mary was herself nursing some injuries and had decided to take a rest the next day. And after that she would walk more slowly. It was a good match.

In a nearby restaurant we were seated at a large table in a back room. Our waiter was hyper-hilarious—a Spanish version of Robin Williams—coaxing us into frequent laughter. He slyly persuaded us to try more entrees than any of us planned or needed. We all knew we had been manipulated by the waiter, but he was so charming about it that we did not mind. We enthusiastically indulged in hearty helpings of various *tapas* (appetizers)—fish croquettes and shrimp pâté, along with succulent green olives. And we hungrily slurped tangy gazpacho soup.

As a pastor, I often saw that meals could mend and renew. The congregations I served were brilliant at potluck therapy. Here in the Burgos restaurant, I could feel my soul soothed, even as I remained unsure about my soles themselves.

It had started as the worst day so far. But now I knew why there was no place I'd rather be and nothing I'd rather do than this pilgrimage. It was not just the extraordinary table companions but all the company of pilgrims who had made this journey or journeys like it before me.

2

SEEKING GOD'S HOMELAND

Christian Roots of Pilgrimage

They confessed that they were strangers and foreigners on earth,
for people who speak in this way make it clear that they are seeking a homeland.

HEBREWS 11:13-14

A GREAT CLOUD OF WITNESSES

On the day that I most dreaded, I found companions who consoled me. Even though they were not always visible, their presence was vital. This became especially clear when I most needed such reassuring knowledge.

My wife, Lorna, accompanied me for the first ten days of the pilgrimage. She could get no more time off work than that and did not feel the same need as I to walk the entire route. She helped me pay attention to things to which I might have been oblivious—the glorious profusion of flowers along the way for example. She particularly reveled in the spacious vineyards we passed through, often with clumps of roses cultivated at the end of rows that only passing pilgrims could see and savor. We marveled at vast plantings of asparagus, all shrouded in plastic so that the tender plants would remain white—as Europeans prefer—and not turn green. There was much to discuss together.

I was grateful that Lorna was able to have a small taste of what this pilgrimage was like, to see some of the scenery, to meet other pilgrims and even to get a little acquainted with companions who would become special to me. We both found the daily challenges daunting and encouraged and supported each other on our way. We had just celebrated our twenty-fifth wedding anniversary and this pilgrimage seemed a fitting reminder of that journey too.

As much as I enjoyed our time together, one sad reality loomed large. With each passing day, I knew her departure was nearer. When I thought about her leaving, I felt a sore and hollow spot in my stomach. I knew I would miss her when she was gone, all the more so because we'd had such an enjoyable trip together.

The dreaded Saturday arrived, and as Lorna and I waited for her bus that morning in the medieval town of Navarrete, the first rain of our journey fell in a light sprinkle. It felt clichéd, but that is what happened. I watched her through the window as her bus pulled away, feeling grief and disbelief. Once the vehicle disappeared from view, I looked for the next sign marking the Camino and trudged in that direction.

On the outskirts of the town I stopped to admire a famous gate leading into the local cemetery. This Romanesque entranceway is strikingly built with four receding sets of intricately carved arches. It is all that remains of an early-thirteenth-century hostel for pilgrims. I snapped a photo and moved on; I was not much in the mood for sightseeing. Soon I was out in the country, wandering paths along parched red dirt fields.

I saw small, strange, sturdy structures of stone atop low hills overlooking surrounding fields. These hive-shaped buildings were about ten feet in diameter. They each had a doorway without a door and a glassless window. No other construction was nearby. I suspected they were shelters for shepherds or other agricultural workers.

I encountered few other pilgrims. I did catch up with Hendrika, an eccentric seventy-something Belgian woman Lorna and I had met a few days earlier in a big city hostel. She'd been talking to herself there and I initiated a conversation with her in Dutch. We were astonished that someone of her age would walk the Camino. She told us that her daughter and grandchildren disapproved, but Hendrika made clear that was *their* problem, not hers. She also told me something that richly rewarded the rest of the trip. She mentioned that the tomatoes in Spain—even ones that did not look particularly pretty or present-able—were especially delicious. Because of her, I ate and savored this fruit every day thereafter.

Hendrika and I visited a little that morning on the path. She moved achingly slowly and I wondered whether she could sustain herself on the journey. I moved on after a bit. I fretted about her, expecting she might show up later at the Nájera hostel, but I never saw her again.

I strode at a steady clip. Lorna and I had taken a day off before she departed, so I was rested. And, sadly, it is easier to walk faster alone. But as the heat built later in the morning and pressed down on me, every-thing took more effort. I tried to rein in my feelings of loss. Once more I felt blisters building ominously, this time on both feet.

I began thinking about acquaintances who were now well ahead of me. I might not see them again because of that day off. As I walked that path in solitude, sweltering in the sun, weary and lonely, I was con-soled to think of Annette and Olaf, Felix and Nichole, Helena and Pi-lar having been there already, even if they were only a day or two before me. Just knowing that their feet had trod the same soil and gravel made a difference. Good folks I cared about had wandered there. They showed it was possible to walk this far. They wanted me to succeed too. "Therefore, since we are surrounded by so great a cloud of witnesses, let us also lay aside every weight . . . and let us run with perseverance the race that is set before us" (Hebrews 12:1).

Millions of pilgrims had gone this way ahead of me in the preceding millennium. I felt an invigorating solidarity with them. One theme for me on this journey was the communion of saints. I was drawn to the Camino by age-old pilgrimage longings. I stepped into ancient traditions.

RESTLESSLY YEARNING AND ON THE MOVE FOR GOD

God is a moving target.

Augustine famously prayed, "You made us for yourself and our hearts find no peace until they rest in you." If so, human nature means that we are always yearning wanderers. We are all homeless, ever since our eviction from Eden. And pilgrimage is an inevitable consequence. We need constantly to look for—and stay on the move for—God.

This search keeps us unsettled. Deity is not easily tied down. Biblical faith is wary of confining divine presence too closely to one place or building, land or sanctuary, race or nation. Faithful people are repeatedly and providentially called to go elsewhere, be displaced and meet—even be—strangers, all in order to encounter our Creator more fully. The tabernacle vividly symbolizes this God of movement, one who dwells in a tent. Bruce Chatwin writes that this

> is a God of the Way. His sanctuary is the Mobile Ark, His house a tent, His Altar a cairn of rough stones. . . .
>
> He leads [the Israelites] out of Egypt. . . . There He gives them their Solemn Feast, the Passover: a feast of roasted lamb and bitter herbs, of bread baked not in an oven but on a hot stone. And he commands them to eat it "in haste," with shodden feet and sticks in hand, to remind them, forever, that their vitality lies in movement.

Journeying, wandering, exile and pilgrimage themes are found throughout Scriptures: the expulsion of Adam and Eve from the Garden; the homelessness of Hagar, Jacob and David; the search by Abraham and Sarah and later the children of Israel for a land in which to settle; Naomi and Ruth's displacements; the deportations of Israel and Judah; the three annual (and communal) pilgrimages to Jerusalem to celebrate Passover, the Feast of Weeks and the Feast of Tabernacles; and the pilgrimage Psalms of Ascent (Psalms 120—134).

These themes unfold in the New Testament with the movements of Joseph and Mary to Bethlehem and then Egypt, the visit of the Magi (the first Christian pilgrims), Jesus' travels with "nowhere to lay his head" (Matthew 8:20). Jesus, of course, names himself "the way" (John 14:6), and that title clearly has implication for how we live. In the Lübeck Cathedral in Germany can be found a lengthy inscription that includes the following rebuke:

> Thus speaketh Christ our Lord to us:
> Ye call Me Master, and obey Me not;
> Ye call Me light, and see Me not;
> Ye call Me Way, and walk Me not.

The Greek word for *way* is related to our English words *exodus* and *odometer*. The metaphor of "the way" is perhaps "the central discipleship motif" in Mark. Alas, we often miss the connection as the frequent Greek term is variously translated as "path," "journey" and "road." Somehow, one of the disciples' most famous arguments is more embarrassing when we know this terminology.

> Then they came to Capernaum; and when he was in the house he asked them, "What were you arguing about *on the way*?" But they were silent, for *on the way* they had argued with one another

who was the greatest. (Mark 9:33-34, emphasis added)

How could they get things so wrong when they were actually en route with Jesus?

Rich implications of journeying and being "on the way" are also carried forward in the apostles' missionary journeys "to the ends of the earth" (Acts 1:8). One author even calls Paul a "walkabout apostle." The New Testament reminds Christians that we are aliens, strangers, pilgrims and sojourners (Hebrews 11:13; 1 Peter 2:11). In Acts Jesus' followers were first known as "the Way" even before being called "Christian" (Acts 9:2; 11:26; 19:9, 23; 22:4; 24:14, 22). That very name captures a sense of ongoing movement. (*Camino*, as it happens, is Spanish for "way.")

All of this is related to the Old Testament use of *walk* to symbolize living morally:

> O that my people would listen to me,
>> that Israel would walk in my ways! (Psalm 81:13)

As John writes: "And this is love, that we *walk* according to his commandments; this is the commandment just as you have heard it from the beginning—you must *walk* in it." (2 John 6, emphasis added).

Journeying has always been a key metaphor for the Christian life.

ON THE MOVE FOR GOD

Pilgrimage in its truest sense is religiously motivated travel for the purpose of meeting and experiencing God with hopes of being shaped and changed by that encounter. Pilgrimages are often concretely physical—journeying to a particular place, perhaps with some extraordinary expense and exertion—*and* spiritual—one hopes to meet God in this travel.

An irony—indeed a danger—of pilgrimage is that we try to settle in a final destination, considering only that particular place holy and forgetting the call to be faithfully on the move for God. Think of Peter wanting to remain on the mountain where he, John and James (*Santiago*) experienced the transfiguration: "Rabbi, it is good for us to be here; let us make three dwellings, one for you, one for Moses, and one for Elijah." His suggestion is dismissed: "He did not know what to say, for they were terrified" (Mark 9:5-6). Christian pilgrimage always calls us to further growth. As Origen wrote: "Travelers on the road to God's wisdom find that the further they go, the more the road opens out, until it stretches to infinity."

Pilgrimage sites are not merely an end in themselves. They are not strictly speaking even necessary. They richly symbolize the fact that our lives are to be a journey with and to God. Even if not all of us can afford or are able to go to famous places for prayer, every time we venture to church for worship we make a small pilgrimage to deepen our faithfulness. The Greek word *paroikia* means "sojourn" and is "also the root of the English word 'parish,' meaning a congregation of pilgrims."

Church sanctuaries usually have aisles that guide pedestrians up to the front. Processionals, offerings, children's stories and rituals invite movement as well. Classic cathedrals have ambulatories, a rounded corridor at the very front of the church (behind the altar), which is literally a "place for walking." Visit such monumental buildings and you almost always find people strolling there.

We sometimes forget the association between church and walking. Most Christians throughout history—and possibly most Christians still—went to church on foot. Old Order Mennonites were not being paranoid when they raised questions about how automobiles would alter church life and in many ways diminish our fellowship.

In the late 1980s I visited a village in the mountains of northeast

Haiti. What I saw on Sunday morning astonished me. People converged on that village from all directions, having walked up to two or three hours to worship in church. They hiked on bare and worn feet over rocky mountain paths. But they wore their finest clothes, and when they got to the town square, they put on their best pair of shoes, the women even donning high heels, to cross the town plaza to the church. For them, church-going is an occasion. They helped me understand its importance. Think of people stuck in poverty—whether in medieval Europe or contemporary Haiti—living hard-bitten lives of austerity, who once a week are invited as pilgrims to feast in God's kingdom. The local church or cathedral was often the only place to encounter beauty and inspiration.

Transformed Understandings of Pilgrimage

Yet over time many Christians lost a sense of the worth of pilgrimage.

Protestant Reformers warned against idolizing humans or confining God to particular places. They denounced a corrupt system of indulgences that offered people time off from purgatory. (Philip Sheldrake argues that the fiercest opposition to pilgrimages came from areas that did not have their own local shrines!) Yet significant benefits were lost in this rejection. For example, it was centuries before many Protestants understood or took up the challenge of bringing the gospel "to the ends of the earth."

Even so, not all pilgrimage traces entirely disappeared. John Bunyan, a seventeenth-century Puritan, famously titled his classic *Pilgrim's Progress*. After the Reformation, pilgrimage came to be understood less and less as an external experience and more and more as an internal journey.

My spiritual forebears, Anabaptists (a category including Mennonites, Amish and Hutterites), never practiced pilgrimage as such. But they knew persecution and wandered extensively, seeking safety and the freedom to live faithfully. For centuries they unconsciously acted in a pilgrimage spirit as strangers, aliens and sojourners on earth.

Such metaphors still inform Christian worship and spirituality; I am regularly astonished by how often *pilgrim* appears in familiar hymns. The terminology is deeply lodged in our hearts, our souls, our imaginations. We Christians see ourselves "as a band of people 'on the move,' searching for the liberation of the world from oppression, wayfarers seeking and getting lost, trusting in the promises and not giving up but struggling onward, an exhausting journey that it seems, at times, will never be completed."

Pilgrimages still happen. Many Christians go to the Holy Land, experiencing firsthand places where Bible events happened and Jesus walked, enlivening their scriptural imagination and understanding. They go for more too. Some tours even offer a renewal of baptism service in the waters of the Jordan River.

Christian pilgrimage centers taking prominence in recent decades include Medjugorge, Lindisfarne, Iona and Taizé. (See appendix three for information about these and other sites.) Foundations that give pastor sabbatical grants marvel at the steadily increasing popularity of such locations. Mennonite tour groups sponsor pilgrimages to places of historical and religious significance in Switzerland, France, Germany, the Netherlands and elsewhere.

Evidence suggests that pilgrimage is being reclaimed and renewed. The Camino de Santiago itself has steadily grown in popularity in the last twenty years. My decision to walk it was rooted in the legacies of many Christians who preceded me.

3

LORD, TEACH US TO BE PRAYERFUL

Spirituality Lessons

—

You trace my journeys and my resting-places
and are acquainted with all my ways.

PSALM 139:2 BCP

BENEDICTINE COUNSEL

I noticed Paul right away. He arrived in the company of several other pilgrims, just as I was hanging up the laundry. The blazing sun and hot wind meant wet clothes would dry quickly.

With my wash done, I had time to observe and study fellow pilgrims. Paul obviously merited attention. Lean, short of stature and his bald head was tanned—he'd walked five hundred miles in the previous month. He wore a permanent crooked smile, one he was happy to shine on everyone. Around his neck was a large but simple wooden cross and around his wrist a woolen Orthodox prayer rope. He greeted all he met, speaking with each one, whether in French, Dutch, English, German or Spanish. He frequently burst into song and invited others to join him. He was winsome, and I could understand why pilgrims were drawn to him.

I felt even more affinity when I learned that he was Dutch. His accent reminded me of my parents and of Henri Nouwen, my spiritual father. We happily chattered in my parents' language. And then, even better, I discovered him to be a Benedictine also. As a Benedictine oblate myself, I decided to ask him about something that troubled me. As much as I prepared for this venture, there was an important question that I could not answer beforehand. I wanted to be serious about praying; it was a pilgrimage after all. One Dutch word for pilgrimage is *bedevaart*, which connotes a prayerful journey. But I was not able to anticipate precisely how that prayer would happen.

I was worried about honoring my commitments as an oblate en route and took this encounter with Paul as providential. An oblate takes lifelong vows to honor Benedictine values as best one can in daily life and to remain accountable to a particular monastery. Many oblates are Protestants; the most famous example is Kathleen Norris, who wrote *The Cloister Walk*. I asked Paul's counsel and inquired how he observes his morning and evening prayer obligation. He told me he had modified his daily devotions and now prayed memorized psalms (for decades he'd chanted dozens daily), recited the Jesus prayer and observed silence while underway. These all seemed good suggestions.

Yet questions remained. Would the demands of a pilgrimage affect what I could do? Would there be enough privacy and solitude in hostels for prayer in the early morning or late day? Would companions influence my practices? More importantly, would I be deepened in Christian life and faithfulness? Would I be taught by God along this way?

PRACTICES OF PRAYER

My disciplines were most affected by whether or not I kept company with anyone else. When Lorna traveled with me, being a good companion was my highest priority. On those days I did little overt praying while walking, although I quietly held up to God people on my prayer list. Usually Lorna liked to nap after we arrived wherever we stayed each day and that was my opportunity to ponder Scripture, pray with my prayerbook and read the Bible and a volume by Teresa of Ávila.

I made use of a handcrafted wooden rosary given to me by a friend. A nonpracticing Catholic, he had no need for it and was unaware that most Mennonites—indeed many Protestants—are leery about rosaries. Such prayer beads were once called *paternosters* (literally "Our Fathers") because they were a way of encouraging people to pray the Lord's Prayer. So I did an entire rosary cycle, praying the Lord's Prayer fifty times. Actually, I chanted it quietly. I also sang a cycle each of songs: "O God, make speed to save us; O Lord, make haste to help us" (a Benedictine version of Psalm 70:1); a favorite from Taizé, "Bless the Lord my soul"; and the Doxology, "Praise God from whom all blessings flow." I also tried to reconstruct, with mixed success, hymns or songs that have been meaningful to me. All the singing was paced by the rhythm of my feet and walking stick. After Lorna departed, I kept up things I had done before but added a few disciplines as well. I usually left early in the morning, before the sun rose, and found myself alone on quiet paths. This opened up possibilities I was eager to explore.

These disciplines were affected by whether I was alone or had company. If no one was around, I sang out loud. If people were ahead or behind, then I might still use the rosary but chanted quietly.

Two significant disciplines I could do whether or not I was alone. Every day, I prayed for my list of family, friends, colleagues, church members and folks with special needs. I also lifted up those who spontaneously came to mind. Paul said he'd heard a cuckoo each day on his travels, so I offered prayers for him when I encountered that bird's haunting call. No matter how far out in the countryside I was, I frequently heard bells, either regular resonant ringing from church towers or the erratic tin clatter from around the necks of grazing cows and sheep. Regardless of the source, these peals were also a call and re-minder to pray.

As well, since pilgrimages represent life's journey, I decided to re-view mine. Each day, I examined a period in my life and talked it over with God. I conversed at length with God about whatever thoughts arose; actually they were mostly monologues from my end, but so it goes. (I also, by the way, developed a habit of talking aloud to myself, which was quite awkward when I returned home!) In many circum-stances I imitated Anne Lamott's two basic prayers, either "Thank you! Thank you! Thank you!" or "Help me! Help me! Help me!"

At first I felt guilty that devotions were affected by my situations. Couldn't I be more disciplined? Shouldn't I be so? But in my own life, even as I have attempted to be prayerful for decades, such practices were appropriately influenced by other circumstances. How I pray as a middle-aged professor with young adult children is different than how I did so two decades ago as a pastor with little ones at home. As a spir-itual director and professor, I often help people find the best way to pray in their own particular setting. The point is not to be onerously and rigidly legalistic but to find life-giving means of paying attention to God and orienting lives toward God in the here and now.

Church Father Clement of Alexandria famously described prayer as "keeping company with God." That's one of my favorite definitions. Walking the Camino was an embodied experience of such companion-ship, one that informs my regular life back home as well.

FLECHAS AMARILLAS AND DISCERNMENT

Living in God's company and by God's priorities is of ultimate worth, but how to do so can be complicated. I was intrigued by the range of indicators—hikers call them "blazes"—marking the Camino and pointing pilgrims in the way to go. They reminded me of many possibilities and dilemmas in discerning God's directions.

Some blazes were small, multicolored rectangles. Different regions of Spain had official yard-high concrete monuments with various stylized shells. (Shells are a traditional symbol of the Camino.) Some cities had scallop shapes subtly etched into the pavement. Those were especially hard to find.

The most common blazes were *flechas amarillas,* yellow arrows casually painted on signs, trees, curbs, houses, fences and even cemetery walls. Imagine the protests about property rights if someone tried to do that here. Trusting these signs takes faith. They look haphazardly slapped on. It would be easy for mischief-makers to create false indicators. (In Ontario I like to hike the Bruce Trail, but some people resent hikers and thus, in certain areas, local property owners occasionally and deliberately tamper with blazes to mislead walkers.)

In cities yellow arrows sometimes were few and far between. I never knew where to seek them: up on a store wall or painted below on a sidewalk or curb. Lorna enjoyed city blazes most. She said they were like a code for scruffy pilgrims as we passed through, much the way hoboes used to leave secret signals to each other about good places to find handouts and shelter. We assumed that pilgrims concentrated hard on the blazes and that city people overlooked or did not even notice them. Yet whenever I felt lost, I only had to ask locals, *¿Donde esta el Camino?* and they promptly and enthusiastically indicated the way.

The markers that most amused me pointed two different directions at once. Pilgrims then would stand and have long discussions, trying to make a decision. Once this happened when I was with a Spaniard, two French people and a German. We carefully consulted our maps and guidebooks in various languages; each book might give different counsel. The most pressing question for us was, "Which way do you think is the shortest?" Then we decided—guessed, really—and off we went.

When alone, I sometimes found it stressful to keep watching for blazes. It was far more relaxing to walk in a group where several people paid attention. This was a reminder of the benefit of community for living discerningly.

A particularly lazy discernment was just following a group and letting them do the work. But I could never be sure they knew what they were doing or even for that matter whether their intention was to be on the Camino! That was a risky way to go, and it is not particularly recommended in Christian life either.

Some of my scariest moments were when I did not see a blaze for a long while and just kept following the apparent route. But what if a marker had been missed? Still, I never got seriously lost and hardly ever went more than a block or two in the wrong direction. If I did have to look longer than usual for a blaze, I'd quietly whisper "Thank you, Lord" when I finally found it.

Another unsettling experience was walking early, in the dark before the sun rose. Blazes were hard to see and find, even with a flashlight. That could be nerve-racking; thus encountering other pilgrims on the same route was especially reassuring.

I wonder what it would be like to have God's will neatly laid out for discernment with vivid *flechas*. Why the constant work of prayer, journaling, Scripture reading, pondering, consulting with fellow believers? And then often we still are not sure that we have it right! But even here, while matters were clearer, there was much discernment required.

On the Camino, as in Christian life, mostly I had to keep paying attention. Sometimes I had an instinct for anticipating the next blaze. The only moment to relax was when I saw a marker, a confirmation, some distance ahead. I could move toward it confidently and not worry for a little while. But once there, it was time to pay attention for the next sign. Discernment is like that too. Ongoing alertness is almost always required.

PROVIDENTIAL ENCOUNTERS

Part of my pilgrimage discernment included paying attention to dreams, which were more vivid than usual. Once I slept in an old, former monastery that had hosted pilgrims for centuries. Not surprisingly, I dreamed about cloistered grounds, labyrinthine buildings and encountering mysterious monks. At one point a character who looked a lot like Brother Paul spoke about the life of faith and quoted a wise mentor as teaching, "See God at work in all things."

That refrain stayed with me long after I woke. I pondered it all day and often thereafter. It rang true and was theologically satisfying. It does not say that God is in all things, some static or inert presence. It certainly does not claim that God is all things, the heresy of pantheism. Nor does it assert that God wills all things to happen precisely as they do; ever since my sister died at age seventeen I am reluctant to accept that idea. But I can look for God at work in all things, at all times, in all places. No matter how bad the situation, God does not give up, despair, abandon us. God is there, conferring hope and help.

I was given these dream words shortly before my bloodied blisters landed me in the ER. Very soon, of course, I saw God operate through those who supported me during that painful time, and I heard God helping me understand that I needed to be more careful about pace and balance.

God is at work in all things.

I came to trust that providence often had a hand in the people I met. I encountered exactly the right folks when I needed to do so.

I was astonished by numerous noteworthy experiences of synchronicity. One evening I stayed at an old monastery in a remote village. The rooms were crowded and poorly lit, so the only place to sit was outside around tables set up in a dusty courtyard. The wind blew and the mountain air was chilly, so we hoped visiting would warm us. I conversed some with Theresa, a Canadian who had greeted me a few days earlier. I had passed her as she sat drinking coffee at an outdoor café; she responded to the Canadian flag on my pack. Now, in our first extended conversation, we discovered that we'd lived in the same city for some years and, even though she is of a different faith tradition, she knows some of my Mennonite acquaintances. Otis was at the table as well. Eighty years old, the retired Episcopal bishop was making this pilgrimage for at least the third time. As we visited, I learned that he had often been to St. Gregory's Abbey, the Anglican Benedictine monastery where I am an oblate, and he knew a number of the monks I count as my confreres. Such pleasant surprises happened semi-regularly, and I did not regard them merely as flukes. Many books about the Camino claim that it is a place of frequent coincidence and serendipity.

Often in restaurants, owners directed pilgrims where to sit. On our third night my wife and I were instructed to be across the table from an East German couple, Annette and Olaf, whom we had seen and smiled at several times in a *refugio* (hostel) and along the path, but had not gotten to know. We made careful conversation over our white bean soup, pork and roasted red pepper, and packaged custard. We discovered much in common, including the fact that our children are approximately the same age. We enjoyed their company and spent a fair bit of time with them during the next few days. But it was the apparent randomness of the restaurateur's directions that made it happen.

Another day I started walking early one morning and encountered a Spanish woman, Rosa, whom I had spoken with several times. We had not planned to accompany each other, but walking the same pace we soon fell in step together and began conversing. We covered a lot of ground in two hours. When we came through a little village she saw a *refugio* and announced that she needed a break and went in to take care of herself. I was happy to shrug off my pack, pull of my boots, drink some water, sit on a nearby bench and rest. I was astonished to see two friends, Chandon and Mary, walk out the *refugio* door. If I had been five or ten minutes earlier or later, we would have missed each other. They said that the next day they would be outside the main *refugio* in Burgos. I resolved to try to meet them. As it turns out, that was where an emergency room nurse ordered me to take at least one day off from walking, a story I've already recounted. Without this seemingly chance encounter, we may have completely missed each other in Burgos, and I would not have had the supportive companions who helped me walk at a slower, healthier pace and who provided precisely the right tonic of companionship for continuing my journey.

After traveling several weeks—by then alone again—I came one scorching day to a *refugio* in Mansilla de las Mulas, around noon. The combination of heat and distance to the next available hostel meant it was best to remain there. During the afternoon I wandered the streets, stretching my legs after a nap. A few blocks from the *refugio*, a thirty-something couple were drinking coffee at an outdoor table in front of a café. I had seen them a few times—the night before they'd been among the eight people who'd shared a room of bunk beds with me. But, until then, we had exchanged only a few words. We knew little more about each other than countries of origin and where we began walking.

"May I join you?" I boldly inquired.

The man extended his hand and pointed his lit cigarette at a nearby chair.

From there the three of us spent a long, leisurely time together that day, talking and drinking coffee. Later in the *refugio* we shared a supper that my new friends cooked. I admired their ability to use savory Spanish tomatoes and create from scratch a sharp and tangy sauce for our spaghetti.

Our conversation challenged me. These companions represented a decidedly nonorthodox point of view; they were not Christians and were fascinated by New Age ideas. And I am a decidedly orthodox Christian. Even so, I was ready to listen respectfully. It was after this conversation that I began suspecting that God wanted me to learn something new. I saw God's providence in how things came about. If I hadn't been by myself and thus available for company, hadn't already been a little acquainted with them and thus had the courage to invite myself to share coffee, didn't have the free afternoon and had not already been listening for some time to people with unfamiliar religious ideas, I might not have heard these folks at all.

In the days that followed I realized that that conversation was perhaps the first time I had listened carefully and respectfully to people who professed to be "spiritual but not religious." I admired their pining for God, valuing of authenticity, seeking of balance and commitment to virtue. I gradually concluded that one of the primary messages God wanted me to receive on this trip was to take contemporary seekers seriously.

I had many moments on that journey where I'd think *what if*—I had been a few minutes earlier or later, I had not walked to that village but gone to the next one instead, I had not randomly chosen that direction to look for a lost hat. And time and again I am struck by seemingly small decisions that led to meeting the very people I most needed to see, the ones God wanted me to encounter.

This too was all part of keeping company with God.

4

—

YOUR PACK'S TOO BIG

Simplify, Simplify, Simplify

—

Make me to know your ways, O LORD,
teach me your paths.
Lead me in your truth, and teach me,
for you are the God of my salvation;
for you I wait all day long.

PSALM 25:4-5

EVERY OUNCE COUNTS

By my third day of pilgrimage I already began violating one of my most important values. I took my Swiss Army knife and sliced up two books. I normally try to keep books immaculate. I don't write in them or fold down pages. I often hesitate to lend them to others, even though that's a sin against Christian generosity. I love books and treat them with great—let's face it, exaggerated—care. Even some family members hesitate to borrow them from me because I am so fussy. But here I was, butchering two volumes.

I carried a thousand-page novel and a small guidebook. But I was faced with a difficult decision. Could I sustain their weight day after day? It did not take long before I knew. As I read a chapter in the novel or passed places described in the guidebook, I tore those sections out and threw them away. This went deeply against my grain. (Others also confessed to me the guilt they felt for similarly defacing books.)

I should not have been surprised by my weight problems. Lorna and I began the pilgrimage in the charming French town of St. Jean-Pied-de-Port, a small, stone enclave still surrounded by its medieval walls. We arrived there after a transatlantic flight, another flight within France and rides on a bus and a train. When we put on our packs on Wednesday morning, we knew our pilgrimage was about to begin in earnest. Until then, it had been all theory. I'd read books and articles and consulted Internet resources, but I'd not actually ever talked face-to-face with anyone who had walked this route. At the train station and on the train itself, I'd glimpsed folks who looked like prospective pilgrims, but I had not conversed with them either. So once in town, we labored up steep, narrow cobblestone streets looking for the Camino office. Two volunteers there, aging but energetic men, warmly welcomed us and showered us with advice. They seemed as enthusiastic to speak with us as we were to meet them. We were grateful for their attention and glad to bring our questions.

Then, however, they gave me a sobering examination, pulled out a scale, grabbed my pack and roundly scolded me—with an expressive French version of "Tut! Tut!"—pronouncing my bag much too heavy. "You'll never make it to Santiago like this," they warned.

The jazz musician Fats Waller used to sing "Your Feet's Too Big." That part of the anatomy is of particular interest for hikers, but these kind Camino volunteers were not looking at my "pedal extremities" (as the song calls them). Foot size is not within my control. Rather, they wanted me to consider carefully what I chose to carry.

An early and perpetual lesson of my Camino sojourn—simplify, simplify, simplify—ought to affect me for a long time to come.

Take No Bag for Your Journey

The day before I departed on my pilgrimage, Matthew 10 was read and preached in our church. There, Jesus instructs disciples, including James, before sending the Twelve on their initial missionary outing. "Take no gold, or silver, or copper in your belts, no bag for your journey, or two tunics, or sandals, or a staff; for laborers deserve their food" (Matthew 10:9-10).

They were not going on a pilgrimage precisely, but there were parallels in Jesus' counsel for me to ponder in my journey. In one of those "coincidences" that happen often in the spiritual life—and especially on the Camino, it seemed to me—the verses spoke tellingly and directly to my situation: travel lightly, graciously accept hospitality, don't hold grudges, be graceful and grateful in representing the reign of God. Tall orders, but worthy ones all. Good guidance for any pilgrim.

Medieval pilgrims honored the spirit of this text. They often carried no food or money, but relied instead on the generosity of others. They might not bathe or bring a change of clothing. No wonder the Santiago Cathedral built a pit to burn pilgrims' clothes—on the roof to get the fumes as far away as possible! That edifice also has one of Christianity's largest censers to dispense pleasing fumes in worship. In most churches those are carried and swung by one person, but the *botafumeiro* in Santiago is the largest in the world and takes up to eight people to lift and wield it. All to mask the odors of pilgrims who had not bathed for months!

As I prepared for my pilgrimage I assembled careful lists of what I would need, and I kept weighing accumulations. (Unlike my pilgrim forebears, I included shampoo, soap, laundry detergent and a change of clothes; I did not intend to need that incineration pit.) Somewhere I read that thirty pounds was a good goal and aimed for that, although once I was in Europe people kept telling me that my bag was too heavy and I ought to cut down to nineteen or fewer pounds!

People commonly do carry too much. Most folks I met regretted the weight they had. I know I did. Some had ten or twenty more pounds than I. Mike was a young Canadian whose fifty pound pack included a can of maple syrup; he hoped to have a pancake breakfast along the way. That was too nationalistic for me, even though I am also a Canuck. People lightened loads as they went, leaving items behind in pilgrims' shelters or mailing stuff ahead to Santiago or back home. (When Lorna departed after a week and a half, I sent a number of things with her.)

As usual when traveling, my hardest decision was how many books to carry. I brought a Bible, *Don Quixote* (Spain's most famous novel), a volume by Teresa of Ávila (it seemed a good time to read this noteworthy Spanish saint), a prayerbook and a guidebook. I kept second-guessing my choices but used all of them along the way. I did not follow Jesus' simplicity guidelines literally. I did have good walking gear and a staff, in spite of the Gospel warning. And while I brought no actual gold or silver, I carried bank and credit cards. I tended not to have much cash on hand, but I always had ready access to sufficient money. I never needed to beg.

Even so I found Jesus' counsel challenging and instructive. While preparing, I heard the line "every ounce counts," a warning against taking too much and an encouragement to be discerning about what to carry. Not only backpackers need to take this seriously. I—and many Christians I admire—often feel conflicted about possessions.

Such concerns are always worth attention, not just while walking five hundred miles. I once taught a seminary course called "Embracing Abundant Life, Unlearning Consumerism" that mightily challenged us to reflect carefully on what we own and what influences pressure us to have more and more. The students and I resisted an assignment to count our clothes, compact discs, videos, books, sports equipment and appliances—and then were stunned to realize how much we possessed. We did not want to know.

The Camino pressed such questions. Managing with a few items carried on one's back makes a person wonder about all our stuff. Simon, a young Swiss architectural student with a lopsided grin and curly cloud of hair, told me that living out of a backpack for a month convinced him he can exist more simply. When he went home he fully intended to divest himself of many possessions. Every ounce counts.

I started thinking about boxes in my basement that have not been opened since my last move, several years ago. Did I really need what was in them? And if I disposed of those, what else could be shed? A couple years ago my friend and colleague Mary was unsettled by how hard it was to move a relative. So for months one of Mary's spiritual disciplines was to give up and give away an item a day from her own household!

For me, all this is easier said than done. The Bible speaks of "sin that clings so closely" (Hebrews 12:1), and I love stuff, especially if it's mine. Even though my pack was heavy, I was still reluctant to surrender things. For example, I had insect repellent that I never used once but did not want to leave behind. I had paid for it, after all, and hate wasting money. I clung to that bottle just as I clutch so many possessions, thinking they too might come in useful some day, but overlooking their toll in the meantime.

The first account of James shows him—with his brother—leaving behind work, nets, fish, livelihood and even his father. It's a theme that keeps coming up in the Bible. As Robert Ellsberg notes, "Whether it was the apostles . . . who abandoned their fishing nets on the shore, or the would-be-disciple who was told to 'leave the dead to bury the dead,' or the adulteress who was forgiven and told simply to sin no more, there were none who followed Jesus without leaving something behind." The Gospel story that most implicates and frightens me is the rich young ruler who at one level wanted to follow Jesus but could not let go of his wealth. Jesus utters a warning that is particularly pressing for affluent Christians, of which I am one: "How hard it will be for those who have wealth to enter the kingdom of God!" (Mark 10:23). Possessions can hinder us from God's reign.

I understand that caveat a little differently because of the Camino. When those two French volunteers criticized my pack, they were not doing so in a judgmental or patronizing manner, certainly not from a sense of exclusionary self-righteousness. Rather, they were genuinely concerned for me and wanted to help me on the way. I hear Jesus' Mark 10:23 exclamation similarly. Jesus loves me—as he did that young ruler—and wants to free me from whatever comes between me and the abundant life he longs to give all of us.

TRAVELING LIGHT

On the Camino there was never the slightest urge to fall for the typical tourist temptation of purchasing souvenirs. I might glimpse a possible gift for a loved one, but there was no point in looking even in the most intriguing stores. There simply was no way to carry anything additional. I bought only food and blister supplies, and these were used up as I proceeded.

We backpackers had a single pressing priority: if at all possible, lighten one's load. It got so that when I went to an interesting museum I debated with myself whether to keep the brochure, even if it had excellent photos. Could I really afford the weight?

This was new for me. I am embarrassed to admit that sometimes in "regular life" when I visit museums, I get almost as excited by nifty shops as by exhibits themselves. In tourism, consuming may replace actual experience. Am I the only one who spends as much or more time and money on mementos to commemorate what I see as I do experiencing and perusing art, sculpture or historical exhibits firsthand?

More and more tourist towns are dedicated to attractive boutiques. Near my former home in Ontario, a person can celebrate Mennonite culture and traditions of simplicity by buying lots of keepsakes in a town with Mennonite associations. Actually, there isn't much else to see or experience. I suppose that if every ounce counts, then there might be some merit in lightening one's wallet as well.

Possessions complicate travel in other ways too. When I journey, I fret about my house and its contents. What if it burns down or the sewage backs up and floods our basement? What if intruders see that we're gone and rob us? I worry about such things until the very moment that I am finally home. So, ironically, even while I'm on vacation, my overabundance of stuff tugs at me and my equanimity.

Belongings, then, always weigh on me at some level, even when I do not carry them on my back. Accumulating goods takes far more time and energy than we ever know. Two rapidly growing industries in North America are closet organizers and storage space rental units. We can even hire consultants and coaches to help us manage our closets.

Lorna noticed that one heavy item we toted was a bag to cover gear during airline flights. Baggage handling is notoriously hard on backpack fabric and straps. When I saw the wear and tear on my rucksack cover after my flight, I was glad I had employed it and spared my pack that damage. But this cover was used only at the beginning and end of the trip and in the meantime had to be carried everywhere. The more stuff we own, the more effort and energy it takes to keep, maintain, insure and protect it.

I would like the Camino lessons to reshape how I deal with possessions.

Out of Sight, Out of Mind

While preparing for this pilgrimage I heard a line: "If you go on the Camino, it's guaranteed that sooner or later you will step in poop!"

Why would one even think that being a godly sojourner is only about edifying experiences?

We walked through many rural areas and saw mushy, smelly byproducts of sheep, donkeys, horses and cows. While I usually managed to avoid treading on it, my luck did not always hold, especially in the mountainous Galicia region. Near the ocean, Galicia is renowned for rain. When paths there—many of them centuries-old donkey and oxcart routes—streamed with precipitation, then fecal matter ran as well, and as the guidebook warned, the inevitable resulted. I wasn't eager for this, but I had to be matter-of-fact about it. Stuff happens, after all.

As an adolescent I lived in the country, and before teaching at the seminary, I pastored a rural church. So I am not as adverse as some to the sights and smells of farms. But several companions objected loudly. They were stunned when I stopped in a little village and perched on a small stone bench outside a dark and dingy bar to eat lunch. For them the local fumes were too bad to consider such a thing, and they kept moving while I sat. As I dined, a dozen cows casually strolled down the main street, drank from the village fountain, and then turned and headed back up the road. Of course, they added to the path's accumulated cattle byproducts as they went.

While I was not thrilled about what other creatures left behind, I pondered how their waste is so much superior to that of cars. I hardly even smell and largely do not see the exhaust of automobiles. Yet each gallon of gas burned in infernal combustion engines generates pounds of harmful substances that go into the atmosphere. These invisible byproducts are far more deadly to our environment than what cattle drop along the way. The fact that we do not have to deal directly with exhaust makes it all the easier to be casual about choosing whether or not to drive.

We need to take responsibility for the effects and consequences of our decisions about possessions and ways of travel, not just what we own but what we leave behind.

I was raised to disdain people who dump garbage on their property, allowing wrecked vehicles or appliances to rust and decay slowly. Good middle-class folks such as I have pejorative labels for "those kind of people." Yet if we had to look at our own waste and its consequences, perhaps we would not be so casual about it.

My sheltered life too often disconnects me from hard reality. Many of my clothes, possessions and appliances are produced by underpaying laborers abroad and overtaxing the earth. And their disposal is often destructive too. Our alienated way of life is one of the most important spiritual and ecological challenges today.

While I enjoy indoor plumbing and miss it when it's not an option, I also know that its convenience—and the fact that I do not have to deal with what goes down the sink, toilet or drain—makes it easy to be irresponsible. Perhaps outhouses should be brought back. Maybe we ought to deal with our own garbage in our own backyards.

One Thanksgiving, our family hosted Fred, a Masai man from Kenya, who was studying at the seminary where I teach. He spoke about how his nomadic fellow tribespeople are not vulnerable to political disruption because they can easily move into the bush whenever the need arises. He told us, "All your wealth and possessions are in this house, but ours are outside." Their investments, he meant, were in the cattle that Masai own. He pointedly reminded us that we North Americans see homes as our own private domain. Of course, our insularity and autonomy is made possible by relatively easy access to technology: heating, fuel, water, electricity, phone and so on. And our sense of independence means we are often concerned only for what goes on in our home but do not worry about the astonishing waste and poisons we put out on the curb, flush down our toilets or let run down our sinks.

Why is it proper to routinely discard items beside the curb—whether garbage or recycling—and allow others to deal with them? As the saying goes, "out of sight, out of mind." Much of what we dispose of has a long half-life. Landfills bulge with computers containing dangerous chemicals. The latest trend is to dispose of toxic-laced PCs—so-called e-waste—when they get too many viruses or junk mail. Recycling is often no more than a conscience-salving ruse. Many cities have recycling programs—often using specially designated blue or green boxes—yet the fact is that numerous items collected cannot in fact be recycled nor do they decay in a timely fashion without further harming the environment.

I would rather not know all this. Then I would not have to deal with frustration every Sunday when I see how much nonrecyclable waste is generated by good Christian brothers and sisters merely so that they can share coffee together. I do not really want to be aware of the toll and cost to the environment when it has to clean and pick up after us. As Aldo Leopold famously lamented, "One of the penalties of an ecological education is that one lives alone in a world of wounds." The more we learn, the more we see how much is wrong and destructive, and too often it feels like others neither know nor care to know.

A small move I made in recent years as a response to all this is being more deliberate about choosing when to drive. I recognize that every time I use a car, I make a theological decision. I need to do this carefully, as an act of discernment. Is this errand worth the strain on precious earth, the use of gas, the wear and tear on this machine? Can I combine this errand with other things that need doing? Can I walk, bike or share a ride instead?

I'm the first to admit that this way of operating is a tremendous nuisance, but in the long run it's healthier for the environment and for me. It's a small irritation that I notice, but a far better one than the larger bother I otherwise cause without seeing its adverse results.

Being a pilgrim means changing one's lifestyle. The Camino was already beginning to reshape how I think about mine. These early lessons shook me up, but there would be plenty of other changes and challenges ahead.

5

—

THE ROAD
THAT LEADS TO LIFE

Challenges of Faithful Pilgrimage

—

*For the gate is narrow and the road is hard that leads to life,
and there are few who find it.*

MATTHEW 7:14

TAKE UP YOUR CROSS DAILY

"Every day is still a struggle and each one requires a recommitment,"
Paul told me, and he was not speaking only of the Camino.

One day, I walked with this Dutch Benedictine, a person of immense joy and warm hospitality. For a few hours we discussed various authors and Christian communities. Of course we sang and prayed together as well.

I asked how a Dutchman ended up being a monk in France. He told me that while he was raised Catholic, he was not devout as a youth. At one point he hitchhiked through Europe. In a remote rural area in France, he needed somewhere to spend the night and ended up at a monastery, with no idea what the place was. While there he unexpectedly had a vivid encounter with the living Christ. He has remained for thirty years, first becoming a monk, later being ordained as a priest.

"That's a beautiful story," I observed, awestruck by this account.

"Yes," said Paul, before adding the sobering counsel about struggle and recommitment.

His words rang true. As a teenager I kept hoping for an ultimate spiritual experience that would clinch my relationship with God and help me arrive instantaneously into full personhood. (For years, I daily prayed in vain for the gift of tongues; I thought that was the key to my spiritual fulfillment.) I worried about the painful growth that was still required of me. And I was continually frustrated at my inability to live up to my own ideals. *Why did the Christian journey have to be an ongoing battle,* I wondered.

Later I became stymied with fear about my incapacity to achieve full Christian faithfulness. I gradually overcame my frustration when I remembered that Jesus counseled followers to "take up their cross *daily*" (Luke 9:23, emphasis added). I took this to mean that I did not have to do and achieve everything all at once. Rather, I just need to be faithful each day in whatever is put before me, the small achievable piece of fidelity God calls me to in that moment. That still requires hard work and daily commitment and recommitment, but it seems ever so much more doable.

I have tried to live in that knowledge for years. While I have a long way to go and grow, I am also amazed by what God has been able to achieve in my life thus far.

The Camino reinforced such convictions. Going on a pilgrimage is a wonderful idea, and when I set out on this trip I could hardly believe this dream was coming true. But from the start it was hard work. Every morning I had to overcome inner resistance and engage the day's difficult challenges once more. The dreaming and planning of the previous year and a half were not enough to get me through it. Every dawn, I faced the ache of muscles again and again.

The road looked tiresomely long, and there were too many hills. I often had reason to recall a proverb I had heard in Haiti: "After the mountains, more mountains!" And I was tempted to rewrite Psalm 23:4:

> Even though I walk through the darkest valley, I fear no evil;
>   because that's ever so much better than tackling yet one more
>   mountain!

It was easy at the journey's beginning to be overwhelmed at the thought of walking five hundred miles. Yet each day I could envision the more manageable daily cross of fifteen or more of them. That was doable. And that I did, day after day, step by step. There was a certain freedom in not knowing everything that was ahead.

UNANTICIPATED RESULTS

Occasionally we start an endeavor with one idea, but something else emerges as vitally important along the way. Some years ago our family decided almost on a whim to hike the Bruce Trail. This lovely route follows the Niagara Escarpment, a rocky ridge with dwindling Carolinian forest in southern Ontario. It's five hundred miles long, much like the Camino. This challenge was no small thing for me in my middle age, as I have never been athletic or outdoorsy. And while I lived almost half of my life near the Escarpment, including all my teen years actually within a mile of the Trail, I was largely unacquainted with this southern Ontario jewel. I thought I was tackling it for a unique physical challenge and as a good family activity. But my wife and children did not enjoy it and stopped accompanying me after the first seventy or so miles, negating the latter motive. And while there were demands, I soon discovered much, much more. This hiking led to a wealth of unforeseen experiences and insights. As T. S. Eliot once wrote in a pilgrimage poem, "Little Gidding":

And what you thought you came for
Is only a shell, a husk of meaning

This commitment fortuitously reoriented my life, facing me with new perspectives and questions that affected my daily mode of travel, choice of church to attend, priorities in shopping and eating and banking, understanding how cities and suburbs are arranged, decisions about recreation, and on and on. I thought I took on a temporary challenge; instead, the Bruce Trail permanently converted me in deep and surprising ways.

As it happens, the year I began walking the Trail, I read a lot about the Camino for the first time and could not understand its appeal. *Why would anyone want to do that?* I wondered. That seemed beyond imagining. But the Trail is the biggest single factor in changing my perception. Gradually I was drawn to the idea of walking the Camino.

Happily, I was better able to do the pilgrimage because my legs had been hiking for years. The Trail made that possible. Within a month of completing the Camino, I traveled to Ontario and finished the last fifty miles of the Trail as well. I hiked easier because of my pilgrimage. So the Trail led me to the Camino, and the Camino led me back to engage the Trail better.

In a few short weeks I also saw the Camino produce unforeseen consequences for others and me.

A *peregrino* (pilgrim) told me that although at first he saw this journey as a hiking holiday and did not intend it to be religious, he was still shocked that much of the time felt so secular. But then, to his surprise, a spiritual agenda grew more and more important to him.

As the old Spanish poem says: *"lo hace camino al andar"* or "the way is made by walking." On the Camino, engaging the route converted us, even when we were not sure that we needed such reorientation.

SLEEPING ON IT

Still, there were challenges. An ongoing hurdle was quality of sleep. Rest was essential. Pilgrims who had a bad night suffered as they tried walking the next day.

While *refugio* hospitality and pilgrim companionship were impressive, sleeping in a room with many strangers, sometimes dozens or more, is not the most relaxing way to go. I had been warned that some pilgrims did not bathe and that the odors also affected sleep. (Once I was greatly offended by smells coming from a bunk mate below me and wondered why he had not washed himself or laundered his clothes, until I later realized in shamed embarrassment that it was not him but my own backpack that reeked!)

It was hard to settle down as I listened to others. Even hearing people sleep peacefully could be disturbing: I envied their steady breathing and obvious restfulness. Normally, we were in tightly packed bunk beds. I often had total strangers of either gender sleeping within two feet of me. Not to mention having others overhead. Many old beds creaked unmercifully whenever someone shifted position during the night. This was especially alarming when the bunk in question was right above and you wondered whether the engineering would hold. And in spite of the fact that I know of no one who had anything stolen, I did fret some about the few valuables I had with me: money, credit cards, passport, camera. I wondered whether they would be safe while I slumbered.

The biggest pilgrim controversy was snoring. The decibel levels of some roommates were impressive. Although I never encountered them, I heard that a few *refugios* had rooms reserved for snorers. The problem there apparently was that people with that affliction seldom admitted to it! Because I sometimes snore, I tried sleeping on my stomach or side (which then adversely affected the quality of my own snoozing).

Even more disruptive, however, was what happened internally. I had vivid dreams and some deeply unsettling nightmares. While no one ever complained to me afterward, more than once I woke myself by yelling out in fear or even weeping. I worried about making a scene.

Several things contributed to an especially rich dream life. With so many intense hours of unstructured, solitary time, there were ample opportunities for agenda to arise and surface, including things I might otherwise ignore, avoid or suppress. I suspect that the physical exercise, especially using right and left legs and arms, stimulated both hemispheres of my brain and perhaps got my mind and unconscious to make new and often startling connections.

The Camino experience jarred loose memories by association. Daily use of various languages touched areas of my life and history. Speaking Spanish, I started dreaming about my first parish where a third of the congregation were Mexican. Dutch conversations sparked me to recall people and events crucial to my heritage and upbringing. French returned me to high school, where I had studied that language.

One night, two of my dreams involved confrontation. In the first, a long-ago friend appeared. Somehow distance had worn away our connections over the years. But I know both of us feel unresolved sadness about that. In my dream he and I were in a boat and he wanted to revisit an unsatisfactory conversation we had had years before. I was paying little attention. He became angry and agitated, in ways that are much unlike him. In the dream I stubbornly refused to engage his concerns and dismissed them as transference. Later, I dreamed about a congregant from a church I had previously pastored. Shortly before I left that assignment, she and her husband stopped attending. We presumed they were upset about something, but they never told us why. In the dream she said that she was finally willing to discuss it. But then she only waffled. That dream also ended in frustration.

After years of regular retreats, I know that idyllic circumstances and beautiful scenery are no protection against painful issues. In fact, they may face us with realities we prefer to avoid. Jesus and later the desert fathers and mothers show that wilderness is not just a place of beauty and solace but also of testing and temptation. In one dream I even encountered a visible Satan—complete with hiking gear!—who was preparing to fight with me as I journeyed for many days in a barren place. Indeed the Camino faced me with my biggest and most troubling temptations: anxiety, competitiveness, drivenness, loneliness and introversion.

While this journey was a pilgrimage, even a dream come true, it continued to challenge me on all kinds of levels. It was not just the taxing work of walking or even the difficult sleeping arrangements. I was not en route to "get away from it all." Rather, the exotic and unfamiliar circumstances, and being free of routine responsibilities, meant I could pay better attention to God. I remember hearing someone once say that God speaks to us in our dreams because that's the only time God can get our attention! A dream about Satan with hiking boots certainly got me to wake up and take notice. More importantly, I was sure that God was teaching and molding me, challenging not just my own internal limitations but calling me to new ways of life.

Why bother with entering unsettling situations, facing and focusing on disturbing matters? Some Christian folks counsel against too much introspection. When my sister died, a minister advised my parents that the best way to deal with overwhelming grief is to ignore it and think about other things. That never worked for me, and it is not something I recommend either.

The Camino, like many retreats, makes issues more stark, sharp and distinct. They are harder to dodge, put off or overlook. In such circumstances it is more difficult to be distracted. In other words, this was an opportunity to spend ample time attending to matters needing processing. Things ignored in the normal routines of life could no longer be overlooked.

A gift, of course, was that these struggles came in a context of readier awareness of God, with time and space to pay attention. That consciousness could reorient me in how I dealt with unresolved issues, matters that deserved more careful consideration than passively sleeping on them.

Easy Yokes and Burdens Light

The day Paul and I walked together was the Feast of the Sacred Heart. The Gospel reading was Matthew 11:25-30, where Jesus extends this reassuring invitation:

> Come to me, all you that are weary and are carrying heavy burdens, and I will give you rest. Take my yoke upon you, and learn from me; for I am gentle and humble in heart, and you will find rest for your souls. For my yoke is easy, and my burden is light. (vv. 28-29)

I took this familiar passage in a new way in the context of the Sacred Heart observance, particularly the phrase "I am gentle and humble *in heart*." I had never paid attention to those last two words before. I would like to know more about the humility of the *heart* of Jesus.

I had often pondered this invitation when I was tired by work, stress or life, and used it pastorally with others as well. Yet I noticed something new. As often occurred during the pilgrimage, I heard Scriptures differently now, simply because I was on the Camino. The Bible opened up in fresh ways. Well-known texts suddenly spoke in another voice with intriguingly new emphases.

As I listened that day to Jesus' soothing words, the language was not merely figurative. "Come to me, all you that are weary and are carrying heavy burdens" speaks powerfully to someone with a weighty backpack, following a pilgrimage trail and hoping to encounter God in new ways. One of the most memorable scenes in *Pilgrim's Progress* is how God's forgiveness entirely releases the protagonist from the weighty load he carried.

Jesus was inviting me to continue on the pilgrimage in full faith that it would somehow come to completion, that I would learn from him, and that I too would benefit from his easy yoke and light burden.

6

THE JOURNEY IS LONG

Camino Confessions

Search me out, O God, and know my heart;
try me and know my restless thoughts.
Look well whether there be any wickedness in me
and lead me in the way that is everlasting.

PSALM 139:22-23 BCP

ALL COMPARISON INJURES

Pilgrimage is often an occasion to review one's life and confess one's sins. This pilgrimage gave me ample time to ponder mistakes and shortcomings in my past. Even more powerfully, the journey faced me with difficult truths about myself, realities that emerged from the intense crucible of an arduous long-distance walk.

For example, while I never competed with others on the Camino, one person did pressure me unmercifully. This one I could not avoid and found hard to resist. I was my own greatest problem.

All my life I have struggled with pace and balance. More than once I plunged into burnout, often connected to my ongoing proclivity and temptation to overwork. A reason that I regularly need to go on retreats is because otherwise my life gets out of whack with depressing regularity.

While on possibly the single greatest spiritual adventure of my life, even here my drivenness manifested itself in sobering and startling ways.

Two times my body dramatically slowed me down, almost bringing my whole trip to a halt. The cause of my emergency room visit was that I walked seventy miles in three days. I wanted to get home sooner after my wife left. My feet were not impressed by this exhilarating achievement. After that imposed respite, I made reasonably good time. But I kept meeting people who routinely seemed to go faster than I. Gradually my daily average crept higher again. Four days before reaching Santiago, I was suddenly afflicted with excruciating tendonitis. While it could be treated with anti-inflammatory cream and alleviated with an elastic bandage, the most important remedy included resting with my leg elevated, taking smaller steps and, above all, walking more slowly.

In the span of one month, I made the same mistake of seriously overdoing it no less than two times. Even for me that's a record in thick-headedness. How does that psalm go?

My wounds stink and fester
    by reason of my foolishness. (Psalm 38:5 BCP)

When I finally reached Santiago, I made a startling discovery. I had allowed myself to be intimidated by guidebooks and folks along the way that said this trip could easily be made in less than a month. I knew that I was not able to do that, but at some level I did not want it to be substantially longer either. Slightly slower, okay, but not too much of a dawdler.

I also felt pressure along the way when I daily saw people who walked farther than I. No one suggested I needed to be like them, but I kept comparing myself anyway. Furthermore, on rest days I knew that familiar people were getting ahead of me and I might not see them again. I did not want to lose pace with my friends.

But in Santiago I was in for a surprise. Not only did I catch up or arrive with people I thought were far ahead of me or faster, I actually got there before some of those very folks! My problem was in comparisons. I kept looking to the minority who appeared speedier. I overlooked many who walked at my pace or were content not to go so fast. And often even "slower" folks arrived about the same time as I. Perhaps I should have reread Aesop's fables along the way, especially the one about the tortoise and the hare.

I was intimidated by people who aimed for twenty-five miles a day. (Later I learned that some of these folks ended up completing their trip by bus.) Or I heard of someone trying to do the Camino in two weeks and self-righteously concluded that that was a marathon and not a pilgrimage: "God, I thank you that I am not like other people" (Luke 18:11). But then I promptly sped up anyway.

I confess that I live much of my life that way too: comparing myself to those who achieve more and greater things. I do so even though I know that this means endless and inevitable pressures. There are always folks in that category no matter what I do or how much I accomplish. I, my feet and muscles, not to mention my soul and soles, would have been far better off if I had just kept pace with and stayed true to myself. As Søren Kierkegaard counseled: "all comparison injures."

HUNGRY, LONELY AND TIRED

Normally I believe that I am independent and self-sufficient, even a bit of a loner. But here I was caught off-guard by unanticipated vulnerability.

In the *refugio* the night after Lorna left, everyone seemed happily settled in their own groups, and no one appeared interested in visiting with a stranger. I was shy about my faulty French and sparse Spanish.

I felt very alone and began pondering the possibility of getting home sooner than originally anticipated; I could walk farther than my prior goal of fourteen miles every day. What was the point of hanging around by myself in *refugios* for hours and hours until bedtime?

On that first solo day, I passed a few pilgrims. I greeted them, but no one responded to my questions. I played hiking hopscotch with a couple of middle-aged Frenchmen, perhaps ten years older than me. Passing each other, we exchanged brief "Bonjours." When one smiled, I tried to engage him in conversation, but he did not seem interested.

The next day, I resolved to walk eighteen miles. (I achieved fourteen by the middle of the morning!) The last four into Grañón were particularly hard. Some of the final stretch was on a highway shoulder where I was not only buffeted by the noise of traffic but transport trucks passed within a few feet. At times their wind threatened to throw me off balance; at other moments I felt as if I would be sucked in by their vacuuming slipstream. The air was blistering, and the pavement radiated heat through the thick soles of my hiking boots. So I was greatly relieved to arrive in the town where I planned to stay, even if it was only noon.

When I got to the center of the village, I was surprised to see the very Frenchmen I had encountered the day before. This time they greeted me warmly, like old friends. And, in French, they plied me with questions: "How are you?" "Truly?" "What was the walk like today?"

I received their attention gratefully. They told me that the little church in town was particularly beautiful, and when I later went to look I had to agree. As they prepared to move on, one indicated a small store nearby and recommended its *bocadillos* (sandwiches). Even though I had packed food, I went in and purchased a lunch. I was that susceptible to suggestion. By the way, I found the purchased food overpriced and not especially tasty! I longingly recalled, in contrast, how a few days before I had discovered a café whose omelet and Serrano ham sandwiches, served with roasted red peppers and fat green olives, tempted me to settle for life at that table.

As I ate outside in the plaza, another pilgrim marched through town. I recognized her from passing her on the Camino yesterday and because we had stayed in the same *refugio* the previous night. Although we had never spoken, other than wishing each other ¡*Buen Camino!* I raised my cold bottle of Coke in salute.

She strode at a purposeful pace but suddenly veered over toward me. She interrogated me about whether I planned to stay the night in that town and then launched into a vigorous and impressive lobbying campaign in energized Spanish. She insisted that I go to the next town, Redecilla del Camino, only another three miles. She argued that the *refugio* there was far better. (Later I met people who overnighted in Grañón where I lunched, and they said this was one of the best and most memorable *refugios* ever!) She noted that it was still early in the day and the next town only an hour or so away.

Even though I was tired—or perhaps because of it—I allowed myself to be persuaded by this friendly face to change my plans. I did move on to the next town.

Later I reflected on what happened. Addictions counselors advise paying special attention to being HALT: hungry, angry, lonely or tired. Although I consider myself independent, even stubborn, I scored three out of four. I was hungry, lonely and tired, and in no time at all allowed myself to be uncharacteristically swayed by unsolicited advice from strangers. Everything worked out fine, but this was unsettling.

I wonder how often day-to-day busyness also leaves me lonely and tired, and thus there too lacking in judgment and discernment.

GETTING HARDER AS ONE GOES

In one of my photos of a marvelous *refugio* meal, people are smiling and laughing, toasting each other and enjoying the company around a long, festively decorated table. But Claude's face stands out. He looks somber and drawn, his face haggard, eyes tired and body slumped. He suffered various physical ailments underway, which only grew worse as he went. He had trouble sleeping, which made walking all the harder. Most frightening, however, was his contention that this journey did not get easier. Instead he insisted that it grew more psychologically difficult as a person neared his or her goal. This was not what I wanted to hear.

In my last week I became acquainted with this fifty-something Frenchman who walked from LePuy, France, one of those hardy souls who did five hundred miles to reach where I only began. I was certainly in awe of him.

Claude's partner, a Dutchman named Willem, also discovered unwelcome challenges. He had come by foot all the way from the Netherlands. And not everything necessarily improved. In fact, he had no blisters for the first 150 miles of walking, and then started getting them nonstop.

I could relate to these two. It was as if I completed the Camino barely in time. The tendonitis in my last four days meant for painfully slow trudging. Several of the most trying treks were in the final week, even as I knew I neared my destination.

I did ultimately make it to Santiago and enjoyed my stay there. But upon arriving I had a chance to go slow, relax, nap frequently and take stock of the situation, and my body began to break down distressingly. I was one of the walking wounded in that city, hobbling on even the shortest of jaunts with my hiking staff. Many Santiago pilgrims had bandaged feet, nursed damaged hips or limped. For me there was the tendonitis, of course. But I also had a nasty rash on my shoulders, a result of combined heat, sweat and the burden of the backpack. My hips, which bore more pack weight, also had a rash and were starting to develop open pressure sores. My feet's thick calluses began to painfully crack apart. And during that month my eyes deteriorated, affecting my ability to identify foreign currency or even to read! I pondered the irony that in medieval times folks often made pilgrimages to shrines to receive healing, but I experienced physical deterioration instead.

It was hard to know how to interpret these symptoms. Was it that I had only five hundred miles of stamina, and that I would have been in serious trouble if I had tried to go much farther? That's possible; I would not have enjoyed coping with such eye, shoulder, feet and tendon problems if I was going any greater distances.

Yet I concluded otherwise. I believe my body could have been prepared to endure even a longer trip. But now that I was at the end, it needed a break, even if this meant breaking down. Often I engage in major projects—like the end of the semester marathon at seminary—only to find at the completion that I suddenly get ill with colds or flus.

Walking the Camino was one of the most challenging summers I ever faced. But the year before was even more difficult. I took on a special project for our school, coordinating a major grant-writing process. I've never worked as intensely in my life. I put in six-day weeks, often laboring morning, afternoon and evening. I was at work at dawn and usually was not finished until after dark. At times it felt like I ate, slept and was totally preoccupied with the work at hand. That is not a way of life that I normally recommend. It fed too easily into my unfortunate tendency to workaholism. I did it because trusted leaders at the Christian institution where I work asked me to do so, and I did so knowing that it was temporary. It was a great project, and we successfully applied for the grant, one that enhances our seminary's life, culture and ministry, and I am deeply grateful. But by the end of the summer I was very, very tired. It was several months before I recovered from that tremendous effort.

In some ways, then, the Camino felt familiar. That too was a project that consumed me. I single-mindedly pursued this pilgrimage. I rose when it was dark, often cutting sleep short to get an early start on that day's journey. Meals, especially breakfast and lunch, were completely dependent on my walking schedule. I lived, ate and slept the Camino, much as I did with the grant project the year before. And my body showed the toll.

Claude was right. It did get harder as I drew closer to the goal. But there was never any doubt for me that it was all worth it.

TRUST, TRUST, TRUST

And while I needed to learn difficult lessons on this pilgrimage, there were refreshing graces as well: a call not only to own up to my own limitations but to accept them as a way of trusting God's fuller grace.

On my second day after arriving in Santiago, my destination, I called Lorna from an outdoor phone. As soon as I hung up, I stepped around a stone pillar and stopped and stared in disbelief. There were Aileen and Elisabeth, a mother and her teenage daughter from Florida who we met on our first day. I had not seen them for four weeks. Lorna and I ate with them at our first pilgrims' meal, happy to get acquainted and compare notes. I had prayed for them every day of my journey, unsure they would make it and quite certain I would never see them again. Yet here they were, having bravely overcome great physical challenges to complete the Camino for the second time in their lives. More than one prayer was answered in their achievement and our running into one another. In walking the Camino, carrying few possessions and being vulnerable to circumstances, more than anything I learned to be prayerful. I constantly offered up to God concerns and worries, places that I hoped for resolution and help. But at the same time, I saw God

at work in what was happening. Surely God does not operate differently along the Camino than in the rest of life. But I learned to pay
better attention to God—God's company, God's workings and God's
interventions.

We had a celebratory supper together and enjoyed catching up on
each others' adventures of the previous month. We wanted our picture
taken together with our own cameras and found a suitably picturesque
spot on the street. We intended to recruit passing pedestrians to pho-
tograph us. Elisabeth was reluctant, because she had never allowed anyone to use her special camera.

A couple I did not know passed by speaking Dutch and, using their
language, I asked for assistance. They were glad to do so and eagerly
queried us about our pilgrimage. As Elisabeth was about to teach them
how to use her camera, the Dutch woman showed that she had the very
same one! And he had one like mine. It was a small incident, not actually all that important. Yet I took it as a divine bouquet to remind me
of God's involvement not just with me on the Camino but also in my
whole life. That, along with greater "coincidences"—such as meeting
a Dutch Benedictine on my first day or finding Mary and Chandon at
my lowest moment—kept calling me to trust, trust, trust.

Abundance or scarcity are two modes of perception that crucially
shape our imagination and choices. I know they make a difference for
me. Do I really believe that God is at work, present and able to make
a difference? Can I trust God with my life? Do I live in the security of
such convictions, or am I perpetually fearful and anxious?

Too much of my life is spent worrying about what others may or
may not do, protecting myself against possible hazards, competing for
seemingly scarce resources. I find myself in an endless race for security
and success. But the Camino experience kept drawing me into coun-
terintuitive modes of functioning.

The lessons on this journey were abundant and obvious. Although I have a pessimistic bent, the Camino over and again taught me to trust that God provides sufficient for what I truly need. At home, I was in the habit of not only having regular meals but also a snack within two or three hours when feeling peckish. On the pilgrimage, I ate when I could or when food was available or when I most urgently had need. Sometimes I had nothing for six- or seven-hour stretches and was fine. Not surprisingly, I lost over a dozen pounds on this walk. (My dear spouse says that that was inefficient: walking so far for so few results!) I could spare the weight; in the meantime I learned a healthier way to eat, trusting that there is enough.

My blisters and tendonitis showed that I miscalculated speed issues. I pressed myself to go fast, as if I did not have enough time, but my body steadily insisted on moving slower. My limbs knew best. I cannot complain about when I arrived. I could have relaxed from the beginning, walking slower and more tenderly, and it would likely not have made much difference in my arrival. There actually was no scarcity of time.

I had heard before I went that it could get so busy that *refugios* became overcrowded and pilgrims raced each other to the next shelter. But this was not my experience. Mostly there was plenty of room each night. Toward the end there were two nights when I had a harder time finding a place to stay. But by then I was suffering from tendonitis and in no position to rush and get anywhere earlier than anyone else. Even so, I always managed just fine and was never without lodgings, especially because of the aid of others.

Once I accompanied Violant and Mercedes for a day of walking, the day my tendonitis flared up for the first time. Violant—who calls herself "Vio," pronounced "Bee-oh"—was a kind Spanish pilgrim in her mid-twenties who was on leave from her work with the developmentally challenged. One thing that particularly impressed me about her was her ability to find four- and even five-leaf clovers as we walked. That evening the first hostel we came to was almost full, even though it was large. She gave me the only free bed and went elsewhere to find lodging. She wanted me to rest my damaged leg as soon as possible. I was grateful for her care and generousity, qualities that no doubt stand her in good stead in her own work.

While some *refugios* were crowded, I had a bed every single night. Over and again, this journey urged me to trust, to relax, to let go. Not to be anxious. Not to worry. Not to fret, even in difficult circumstances. A motto I made up for myself when I returned home proves helpful in the face of frustrations: "This is not as hard as the Camino, and I volunteered for that!"

Many Camino pilgrims begin their journey in the picturesque medieval city of Jean-Pied-de-Port, on the French side of the Pyrenees.

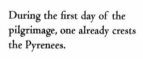

During the first day of the pilgrimage, one already crests the Pyrenees.

Boots neatly shelved in a little hostel in the Pyrenees hamlet of Orisson.

A vista of fields, forests and mountains in the Navarra region of Spain.

The author's wife, Lorna McDougall, visits with Felix, a Dutch pilgrim, in a hostel in Los Arcos.

Pilgrims resting on a street bench outside the Estella hostel.

All in a day's walk in the La Rioja region of Spain.

A statue typically depicting St. James as a pilgrim with the symbolic paraphernalia of staff, drinking gourd and shell. This was in the Santa María la Real church in the city of Nájera.

Many churches depict St. James as *Matamoros*, the Moor-slayer. This statue was located in the Santiago de Compostela cathedral.

Various blazes pointing the direction of the Camino.

This humorous mural, poking fun at overloaded pilgrims, was on the external wall of a hostel in a small village outside of Burgos.

A simple and festive meal in a mountain hostel in Ruitelan, about a week from Santiago and just prior to crossing the final mountain range.

Pilgrims heartened one another by various means. Here someone formed a stone cross on the path to encourage other passersby.

The author in the city of his destination, Santiago de Compostela.

The famous front face of the magisterial cathedral of Santiago de Compostela.

7

WELL, THAT'S THE CAMINO

Hospitality and Solidarity

—

Stand at the crossroads, and look,
and ask for the ancient paths,
where the good way lies; and walk in it,
and find rest for your souls.

JEREMIAH 6:16

REFUGIO RENEWAL

About a week before arriving in Santiago, I had to cross my third
mountain range. I determinedly set out from the city of Astorga
about half past five. In early morning darkness I tapped my way out
of the city, my walking stick's metallic point resounding on the cobblestone streets. I saw only a couple of other pilgrims underway at
that predawn hour.

I was unsure about how far I would try to go that day. Still, I felt
strong and ready for whatever challenges might arise. I quickly
achieved twelve miles, stopping for leisurely coffee breaks at two small
restaurants along the way. In one, I indulged in a newly favorite mid-
morning snack, *tortilla*, a hearty omelet of eggs, potatoes and onions,
all served with hefty chunks of bread.

I arrived at the tiny mountainside town of Rabinal by 11 a.m. Although many guidebooks recommended staying here, and although I understood there were exceptionally enjoyable *refugios* here, I was reluctant to stop, as it was still morning. The problem was that I was not certain when I would next find a hostel. But it was early in the day, and I felt particularly fit.

I knew I would be committed to at least a couple more hours of walking after leaving Rabinal, including a steep climb in the next few miles, the second to last mountain range of the Camino. So I took a long break first before moving on. I visited a small store and bought a lemon Fanta and some nectarines. Resting my body and fortifying my stomach for the workout ahead, I sat on a little bench in the street, conversing with the storeowner and a Spanish hiker. I admired nearby houses, whose lovely stone window boxes brimmed with bright flowers.

The next hour involved a steady ascent. As I climbed, the stillness deepened. All I could hear was the wind, occasional birds and erratic cattle bells. While the weather was not unmercifully hot for a change, it was not particularly comfortable either. The overcast sky provided protection from the sun, but the air was also densely humid. So I did a fair bit of perspiring; combined with a cold wind, I felt clammy. Never once that month did I figure out the best way to dress while climbing mountains.

First I came to Foncebadon, an eerie, abandoned village of gray slate houses, many of them collapsed. But there was a small, working, ramshackle restaurant, and so I promptly downed two more Fantas. While there was a hostel in town, it was only noon and the *refugio* would not open for several more hours. I pressed on toward terrain that guidebooks ominously call "tortuous."

Until now, the day had proceeded smoothly, but I was beginning to tire and my feet had started aching. I had at least another four miles to walk, on a day when I'd mounted the highest peak of the entire journey. The sun was high and there were few trees for shade. In moments such as these, time and distance become relative. The miles stretched achingly. Gnats kept swarming me. The gritty path was dusty.

I passed through still another abandoned village, Manjarín. Here a famous hostel is run by an eccentric and well-known loner, Brother Tomas, who claims to be a latter-day Templar. As I approached along the road, he clanged a bell, his custom for welcoming all passing pilgrims. I stepped over two large hounds flaked out in the baking sun and stopped to visit. He welcomed me to sit in the shade on a picnic bench. But then, for some reason, he refused to speak with me. He sat nearby but never responded to anything I said, his head buried in a book. When two Spanish pilgrims arrived on horseback, he engaged them in vigorous conversation, adding to my sense of alienation. That inexplicable behavior—on top of the notorious and evident lack of hygiene there—convinced me to proceed. The testy Templar did not acknowledge my farewell.

Every time I went over a hill or rounded a corner, I hoped that the next town would loom into view. I began second-guessing my decision not to stay elsewhere earlier. Although heather bloomed along the way and a range of purple silhouetted mountains extended to the far horizon, I was less and less impressed by my surroundings. I just wanted to arrive.

Finally I descended a steep mountainside path into the village of Los Acebos. I was tempted to hurry down, but knew that accidents are most likely at the end of a tiring hike. The town overlooked emerald mountains and valleys. The one main street between the closely packed two-story stone buildings was so narrow, I wondered whether the sun ever struck the pavement. I was glad to be somewhere, but this place was only slightly more appealing than Foncebadon or Manjarín. There were no window boxes here.

I did not know whether there was a *refugio*, but a sign pointed down a side street to a bed-and-breakfast, *La Trucha* (The Trout). By now, I was willing to splurge. The owner paused and chewed his lips. He was reluctant to rent a three-bed room to one sojourner, but it was late in the day, and he knew he did not have much chance for any more clients. I desperately hoped we could come to an arrangement and, happily, we soon did. I felt embarrassed about walking through his house in trail-stained clothes. It took all my strength to climb the narrow flight of stairs to my bedroom. As I mounted the steps, I worried that my heavy pack might knock against pictures he had hanging on the walls.

I could not remember when I had felt as exhausted in the previous three weeks. I had walked around twenty-five miles, up and down, up and down, all day long. As soon as my pack and boots were off, I slept solidly for over an hour, not bothering first to remove any of my soiled clothing.

Then I showered, washed clothes and hung them out to dry. I admired my host's lush, green vegetable garden. I stared back in awe at steep slopes, ranges I'd crossed that day. My host, Rafael, provided me the only vegetarian meal of that month: a superb supper of salads made from his own produce and hearty homemade whole-wheat bread. That evening and next morning, I got better acquainted with him. A meditative middle-aged man, this refugee from the big city opted rather for a simple life of gardening and hospitality. Living with his dogs and cats, he seemed content. And I felt renewed.

HOSPITALITY'S SHAPES AND SIZES

A year and a half later, I can recount in order and laborious detail every place I stayed that month. Shelters included a wide range of facilities: two bedrooms in one half of a privately owned duplex; seventy beds crowded into a windowless stone medieval hospital; cozy rooms in rustic wooden cabins (reminding me of "up North" vacations in Canada); a centuries-old stone house under renovation, where swallows in the upstairs hall flew in and out of the broken kitchen window to get to their nest; massive dormitories in nondescript modern municipal buildings; an old Spanish farm whose courtyard now includes a small swimming pool. The latter seemed a mirage on a scorching day, but it was a veritable oasis. Most were tidy and well tended, in spite of the huge daily turnover of *peregrinos* arriving and departing.

Even more striking was the diversity of hosts (*hospitaleros*). The youngest that I recall was in her early twenties, and the oldest in his late seventies. At least half were Spanish, but a good number came as volunteers from other countries (mostly Europe, but also Australia and Japan). When I first arrived at the end of a day's walk—tired, sweaty and eager to find a bed—these folks were preoccupied with crowd control, formal registration and rule enforcement. That's not surprising, given the huge numbers of people they deal with daily. Usually, if I did not react to the initial gruff officiousness, hosts warmed up and seemed friendlier.

Each *refugio* is uniquely formed by the personalities of those who run it, their sense of humor or eclectic tastes. I never knew what to expect. No two hostels were alike.

In the middle of a small, medieval, stone city, Estella, we pilgrims were welcomed into a coldly official building with congested dormitories and too few small coed bathrooms and showers. While the hosts barely spoke an unnecessary word, they played Gregorian chants over the foyer loudspeaker in the registration area. As we ate breakfast the following morning, however, they broadcast Bob Marley at top volume.

The San Juan de Arcos *refugio* is a deteriorating medieval monastery atop a small mountain at the end of a rigorous eight-mile wooded walk.

The same priest has presided over it for three decades. Every evening he offers Mass and a pep talk. All who attend are then welcome to as much garlic soup, traditional Spanish fare, as they care to eat.

Another priest—fluent in half a dozen languages—ran a hostel near his parish church in Carrión de los Condes. One claim to fame for this town is that St. Francis of Assisi visited there on his way to Santiago. There were lots of rules at this particular establishment. To prevent eager pilgrims from rising early and disrupting surrounding sleepers, no one was allowed to leave their beds. Signs in several languages essentially said, "Don't even think about getting up before 5:30." (It was not clear whether we were allowed to go to the bathroom during the night!) While some places permitted people to take up to two hours to awake and disperse, here the priest started blaring loud church music at 5:30 and then greeted us in Spanish, French, German and English, bidding us to rise "in the name of the Father, the Son and the Holy Ghost." The hundred or so pilgrims dispersed in less than an hour.

A favorite shelter was a house in Ruitelan, a small mountain village. Here we were aware that the next day included the challenge of cresting our fourth and final mountain range. The town was so small that it had no store. But there was a bar across the street with a widescreen TV, where locals watched Wimbledon! Three rooms were set aside in the *refugio* for pilgrims. Some companions and I slept in the spacious attic.

That evening, the *hospitaleros* prepared an ample meal, with abundant water, crusty white bread, wine, watery but welcome soup, various salads, heaping servings of spaghetti Bolognese and custard for dessert. A simple and satisfying supper, all of it homemade. The starchy noodles were particularly valued by long-distance trekkers. The hosts laid out place settings in an attractive and colorful fashion, using old, cracked and mismatched dishes. In the morning they provided a basic breakfast. They bantered jovially with us in many languages, and we listened to rousing music on their stereo system. Even as I knew we faced a daunting climb that morning, their good cheer and warmth were invigorating. We felt energized for the challenge ahead. And the climbing of the mountain was not nearly as difficult as anticipated. We crested in a few hours, the easiest mountain yet. No doubt the hospitable launch from Ruitelan eased us on our journey.

AT TABLE IN THE KINGDOM

Over and again, meals inspired and drew us together in surprising ways.

On our very first day, we stopped at a small but charming hostel in Orisson, about five or so miles out of St. Jean-Pied-de-Port. It was precariously perched on a Pyrenees mountainside and afforded stunning views of verdant valleys.

We arrived early enough to shower, do laundry, nap, pray, write in journals and read. Throughout the afternoon we briefly conversed with other pilgrims, exchanging a few sentences here or there. And like most of the subsequent days of my pilgrimage, I had the opportunity to speak several languages: English, Dutch, French and Spanish. I even ended up translating from French into German (relying on me for this shows that people were especially desperate). There was a friendly atmosphere among *peregrinos*, but not much sense of connection yet.

That evening, however, a dozen of us gathered at a long wooden table for the standard pilgrims' meal the *refugio* staff had prepared: clear soup, roasted potatoes, cheap but well-cooked beef that fell apart under our forks, many loaves of bread, red wine aplenty and yogurt to follow. People soon began nodding and smiling at one another and conversing in whatever common bits of language we could cobble together.

One man, a gifted extrovert fluent in five languages and a vital repository of goodwill, sat halfway down the table. He kept looking around and when someone was quiet too long, he asked a few questions and drew that person in once more. He humorously badgered people to sing in their native tongues. So we heard and sang French, German, English, Spanish and Dutch songs. Many of us knew Taizé pieces too. (See appendix three for more information about this contemporary pilgrimage center.) In following weeks I often sang when I walked alone. And I heard singing in church services I attended. Twice I sang with a partner on the path. This was the only time on the pilgrimage, however, that I experienced a group of pilgrims singing together.

I could feel congeniality growing. Conversations took on depth. We began telling each other our names, as well as important information about ourselves: our lives at home and our hopes, fears and longings about the pilgrimage. Suddenly we were no longer strangers who all happened to reside one night in the same place. Now we were engaged in a common project and interested in how things would go for each other. In the next month I was always especially glad when I ran into people from this very first night. Social philosopher Albert Borgmann writes about the foundational importance of the culture of the table. He speaks of the significance of cooking food, sharing meals as a family and with others, exercising hospitality. All of this is rooted in the central Christian rite, the Lord's Supper. That first pilgrims' meal confirmed Borgmann's insightfulness. Truly, we met God in each other and while sharing food.

As the miles mounted, our schedules and pace varied widely. As time passed, we first-night pilgrims did not see each other as regularly. I often prayed for these folks along the way, remembering their particular fears, hopes and challenges. Some of my happiest moments in Santiago, at the end, were running into people I conversed with at that very first pilgrims' supper. A relatively brief time at table touched and fed our hearts for many days and miles, right until the completion of our pilgrimage. It bonded us.

Meals together were one of the most significant aspects of the Camino. I often find myself recalling where and with whom I ate. I liked—often even loved—the food, but I was most grateful for the company. As Christine Pohl writes: "A shared meal is the activity most closely tied to the reality of God's Kingdom." No surprise, then, that so many New Testament stories—parables about banquets, feasts in homes, the Last Supper, miracle feedings—revolve around food. Twenty-five years ago, a friend named Bill told me something I still often recall: "If you can read the Gospels without getting hungry, you're not paying attention."

SMALL TALK LOOMS LARGE

We also extended hospitality to one another in conversation. An introvert, I find small talk difficult. It requires a great deal of energy. Yet I envy those who do it well and with grace.

Here my usual introverted mode was reoriented. On the Camino I engaged in more small talk in thirty-one days than any other month (perhaps any year!) in my life. After long, lonely hours of solitude on a quiet path, often beginning at half past five, well before the sun rose, I was usually eager for human contact and connection. Many days I did not read a single page—an unimaginable hardship in regular life—but instead opted for chatting at length with others. Even when we did not know each other well, there was plenty to discuss. Often I was too tired to visit and tour famous locations once I stopped walking for the day, but there was always energy to spare for visiting. I began wondering whether important aspects of my personality were being transformed.

I did not necessarily anticipate the earnest and profound heart-to-heart dialogues I like to have with my spouse and other good friends.

That happened sometimes, and I was always grateful, but it was not a necessity. The possibility of communication was hampered by the fact that we frequently did not share a first tongue. We patched conversations together with bits and pieces of whatever language was available. There was lots of smiling and laughter. That can be a good substitute when vocabulary is insufficient.

And so talk was frequently basic. Where did you begin today? How far have you walked? Where did you start the Camino? Are you going all the way to Santiago? Where do you hope to reach today? Tomorrow? Such questions and their responses did not necessarily render deep theological, philosophical and spiritual insights, but they were fruitful.

On a basic level they were a way to connect. While walking five hundred miles was physically and emotionally hard, it would have been much more difficult attempting to do so alone. If I set out to trek a comparable distance here in Indiana and no one else did the same, the task would be infinitely more challenging. One thing that helps us walk the little way to church on Sundays is knowing that our good friend and fellow church member Alan Kreider does so as well.

Trudging through big, busy cities, with cars racing past or well-dressed shoppers strolling the streets, I felt eccentric and strange. There I was, sweaty and carrying a heavy pack with my hand-laundered clothes and smelling in ways even I found problematic. But I was not by myself. We pilgrims were different, no doubt about that. Once, when I sat with others in a hostel courtyard, a steady stream of respectable looking, middle-aged shoppers passed by in the street and stared at us through the fence gates, as if we were zoo animals.

Yet knowing I was not the only oddball on this journey encouraged and sustained me.

On a deeper level, small talk validated pilgrims and what we were doing. It reminded us that we were not solo and anonymous. Little

details connected us, and those little details counted a lot. It was
heartening to compare notes about where we each began the pilgrimage and where we started that day, how far we walked and what our
goals were.

I learned long ago in giving pastoral care that in stressful situations people feel not just severely alone but profoundly misunder-
stood. The sense that "I'm the only one who knows, understands or
feels this" may be even more difficult than whatever appears to be
giving the pain (whether, for example, depression or divorce or failure). It is important to name and share the details and to have someone else listen to them.

A resolution I brought home from the Camino is to work harder at
chitchat. Many people struggle with loneliness and sorrow, often unseen. Plenty of folks wait and long for conversation, even simple, seemingly superficial exchanges. If a few words lighten someone's journey,
then I want to offer such a blessing. Small talk is not necessarily trivial.

THE CAMINO'S PERSONALITY

One particular act of Camino solidarity stands out in my memory.
Young and multilingual Agnes was an agnostic who seemed stunned
when she learned I was—in her terms—a "priest." She started accompanying me to help me find a hospital in Burgos, two weeks into my
trip, as my blisters needed urgent attention. But when she saw how
slowly and gingerly I moved, she explained that she had appointments
to see people, gave me a sketchy map and abruptly departed. She was
in a hurry. Peeved, I plodded on with my solitary search.

A few blocks later she suddenly and inexplicably reappeared, looking for me. Her appointments apparently unimportant, she said she
was learning from the Camino that she keeps herself too busy to honor
her highest priorities. Off we trudged, together again. This time she

stayed with me until the ER nurse, who specialized in treating four or five pilgrims a day, had tended and bandaged me.

People often spoke of the Camino as if it has a personality. The hospitable and convivial spirit of pilgrims and local Spanish people were attributed to it. Astonishing coincidences were credited to this pilgrim's path. "Well, that's the Camino," people remarked over and again.

I heard intriguing theological insinuations in discussions of "the Camino." People personalized, even divinized, this route. They spoke of it mystically, as if it is a wise, caring mentor: "It will teach you what you need to know"; "It surfaces what you must face"; "If you must walk it more than once, you did not get it." An Italian chef, Stefano, wrote from Italy, months after we'd parted, "The Camino works in me . . . step by step."

I did not totally dismiss such ideas. I was deeply impressed by the unique Camino ethos. I can still hardly fathom the sheer number of people undertaking this demanding journey. Amazingly, it all worked well. The mix of many people and hardships certainly could have been a formula for serious trouble. Instead, the experience might almost persuade me to be utopian. Neither competition nor self-protection was needed. Rather, cooperation and collaboration, even trusting complete strangers, were the modes of operation, and they worked well.

I do not know how others made sense of their mystical conceptions of the Camino. It was as if the instinct to believe in something greater than oneself compelled people, even if they resist more conventional faith expressions. As a Christian I am not troubled by the idea that the Camino has personality, character or spirit. That was my experience, and it fits my theology as well. Theologian William Stringfellow long ago showed that institutions and organizations, communities and cities have a spiritual dimension and dynamic, perhaps even their own appointed angels. Why not pilgrimage places and routes as well? In New Testament language, these mysterious realities are "principalities and powers."

People were correct that something spiritually unique was afoot. I sensed it too. But we err by elevating the Camino too much. A pilgrimage route may help someone get in touch with God, but is not itself divine. The Camino's vocation—indeed the purpose of all God's creatures, including angels, dominions, powers and principalities—is to honor God and serve the needs of God's creatures.

The Camino, with its ethos of hospitality and solidarity, lends itself to both possibilities and to priorities of worship and service.

8

No "Ustedes" por Favor

The Rules Are Different Here

Let us go to God's dwelling place;
let us fall upon our knees before his footstool.

PSALM 132:7 BCP

BORDERLINE BOUNDARIES?

One sweltering afternoon I was overtaken by an older Spanish man that I'd seen earlier on the trail (and would never encounter again). We'd exchanged polite greetings a few times along the way before, but we had not conversed.

He seemed friendly enough but then, without invitation, launched into a passionate tirade, loudly scolding and reprimanding me about the problems with my external frame pack, which he considered very bad *(muy mal)*. He insisted that internal frames are more ergonomic and the only way to go. With emphatic urgency, he demanded that when I got to the next big city, I should toss my pack away and buy one just like his!

I was struck by his willingness to express forceful opinions to unfamiliar people. I am not used to folks—let alone strangers—giving such strongly worded and unsolicited counsel. Was it something about the Camino?

Once I was eating delicious octopus, *pulpo,* a Galician specialty, for lunch in a quaint restaurant. The elderly proprietress greeted newcomers at the door as she used an old pair of scissors to shear octopus limbs into bite-size pieces. I sat alone on a wooden bench at a long table. I had my leg propped up with a bag of ice on top of it, trying to treat my tendonitis tenderly. Then in walked a pilgrim I recognized from the trail, although we had not spoken together before. I knew neither his name nor his nationality. Yet I waved him over and immediately invited him to share *pulpo* from my wooden bowl. He took a toothpick and began selecting choice morsels. People, strangers actually, often divvied up food with each other, even to the point of biting from each other's apples and drinking from one another's water bottles. (My wife, a nurse concerned about hygiene, has strong opinions about such behavior.)

In the field of ministry we talk about "boundaries" and their maintenance, and what is and is not appropriate limit-setting. But the Camino had unfamiliar rules. This was partly because Spanish culture is different than my more familiar North American Anglo context. Yet even this observation is striking to me. So much boundary language—including that which I teach in seminary classes—sounds absolute and nonnegotiable. Here we saw that much of it is contextual.

It was not only being in Spain, however. Some exceptional boundaries had to do specifically with Camino life. We slept and mixed in close quarters with virtual strangers day after day. Our rooms were never segregated by gender; there was little privacy. We shared important confidences and dilemmas with each other, relying on people we might never see again. Folks spontaneously poured out their hearts, with long litanies of complaints and deeply personal revelations, often before we ever heard each other's names. It was accepted and even usual to engage unknown people in conversation, get advice and ask direct personal questions.

When people travel, feel lonely and know they may never see each other again, it is easy to let down their guard and share matters they might be reluctant to say to those who are more familiar. We've all had such experiences on buses, trains and planes. But there was more going on as well.

I had to pay careful attention to Camino culture and discern what was and wasn't appropriate. I mixed roles in ways that are unusual and perhaps even ill-advised at home. With some people I was companion, listener, guest, counselor, teacher, minister and evangelist, and at the same time I relished their support, was fed by them and even once received physical therapy on my bad leg.

There was something deeply liberating about being able to relate to people in new ways, even if that at times felt confused and confusing.

Xabi, a young man with a broad grin, quietly befriended me when I was having a bad day during my last week of walking. Later, at a table in Santiago, knowing this would be our final visit before he caught a train home, he told me he had resolved before the pilgrimage to speak to everyone and anyone, regardless of age. I knew this to be true because I witnessed several times his outgoing behavior. He ruefully observed now, however, that the rules were already different at the end of the Camino. That day he'd seen a young woman his age and was about to talk to her, but dared not because he was no longer dressed as a pilgrim and did not know what was acceptable. What was normal friendliness for the last few weeks could now be easily misconstrued.

Happily, I am not aware of vague Camino boundaries going awry. Instead, this unfamiliar freedom felt a lot like the reign of God, the way things can be but all too seldom are.

IF YOU PLEASE

One evening at supper, in the famous medieval pilgrim town of Roncesvalles, I mustered my best French and politely asked Jean-Louis to please (*s'il vous plait*) pass the bread. He stubbornly refused, sternly lecturing me. On only the second night of the journey I had already made a major faux pas, but was unsure what it was.

Jean-Louis was a retired engineer in his late sixties who had walked five hundred miles to get where we only began the pilgrimage, and he had the severely blistered heels to prove it. Lorna and I both enjoyed his company, even if he had a marked preference for talking to her and even if his response to hearing my theological occupation was the Frenchman's equivalent of a raspberry! That seemed ironic: to be derided for Christian service while on pilgrimage.

The substance of his rebuke at the table was this: "There is no *vous* on the Camino. We are all pilgrims."

English speakers are often not accustomed to the fact that many languages (including Dutch, French, German and Spanish) have two versions of *you*. When addressing equals, familiars or people younger or of less status, one uses the informal version. It is a basic measure of politeness to speak to strangers or "betters" (whether by age, class, education, wealth) with the formal version.

Even as one gets acquainted with people of roughly the same status, formal address is vital. Not doing so correctly might cause offense and prompt this kind of retort: "Why do you dare call me *tu*? You do not know me. We are not friends."

At some point, when relationships achieve a certain level of openness and familiarity, one or the other person will say something like: "You don't have to address me that way. Let's be more casual. We are equals, peers."

Jean-Louis reprimanded my formality. Being conventional made sense to me. He was around twenty years older than I and worthy of respect. But he wanted me to know that rules "out there" in the wider world do not apply on the Camino. A slow learner, I received a similar lecture two days later in a hostel at Cizur Menor. This time I addressed Miguel, a long, loud and lanky Spaniard around my age, as *usted*. He emphatically made clear that I ought to call him *tu*. There are no *ustedes* on the Camino, he exclaimed.

Decades earlier in Spain, George Orwell also observed the extraordinary suspension of *usted*. During the Spanish Civil War anarchists took control of a city: "Servile and ceremonial forms of speech had temporarily disappeared. Nobody said, 'Señor,' or 'Don' or even 'Usted'; everyone called everyone else 'Comrade.'" Orwell was ambivalent. While exhilarating, it was also unsettling: "There was much in it that I didn't understand, in some ways I did not even like it, but I recognized it immediately as a state of affairs worth fighting for."

More than one person told me that this unfamiliar informality was liberating. It alleviated a tension that many live with daily, trying to know where one stands in relationship to others. I do not understand what that is like; class in North America tends to be more subtle and hidden. In Europe I always play it safe by addressing most adults formally. If I get it wrong, they usually tell me, and it seems not to fluster anyone. If I am supposed to be embarrassed, I'm not aware of it! Being an ignorant traveler has its perks.

Pilgrimages have always been spheres for folks to mix across dividing lines of culture, age, nation, class, politics, language and ethnicity. Pilgrims—like other groups on the edge of society, even those who are voluntarily marginal—cross boundaries that normally separate. Pilgrimages resist hierarchy and structure; folks temporarily suspend regular roles. Simplified dress codes, strenuous challenges and pared-down lifestyles, in the context of a supportive community, all contribute to what anthropologists call "liminality." This describes a betwixt-and-between state that can help convert people from one way of life to another.

All these conditions were certainly true for the disciples as they walked with Jesus and also for those of us on the Camino. James, *Santiago,* and his brother John craved status. They once asked Jesus whether they could sit on his right and left hand in glory. This occasion became for Jesus an opportunity to remind his followers to be different than the world, unlike the Gentiles. Rather than lording it over others, we are invited to be servants of each other (Mark 10:35-45).

It made sense that distinctions elsewhere did not necessarily apply on the Camino. Sure, we might be blue or white collar, middle class or well-off. True, we were different ages. But now we were also notably similar. All of us were on a comparable quest, with corresponding struggles. We shared bathrooms and bedrooms, where we slept in numbered beds in close proximity to one another. We lived simply and sweated profusely. Just as the Camino was not a place of competition, nor was it a place of status. Our only rank was our strong odor. Here there was no hiding behind social designations or distinctions. That too had a Gospel feel.

I smiled and nodded politely at Jean-Louis's harangue. It's a stance I've often found useful as a pastor and professor. Once he was done his speech I waited and waited, but no bread was forthcoming. So I reiterated my request, this time adding *"s'il tu plait."* Only then was I rewarded with a baguette.

SHARING SUCCESS

At one pilgrim's hostel, we were offered a fortuitous bonus. Hosts from the next *refugio,* in Puenta la Reina, fourteen miles farther, were willing to pick up some of our possessions and transport them by truck to the next night's destination. They would not take our entire bags but would allow us to send ahead selected heavier items.

Were we "authentic" if we took advantage of this offer? I worried about that a little, but we were sore and tired from our walking with weighted packs and were suffering from this unaccustomed way of living. I did not fret too long. We happily accepted the proposal.

And we shared this possibility with other pilgrims. Olaf and Annette had not heard about this service. We wanted them to benefit too. My cynical side ponders whether I hoped others would alleviate my guilt about potential compromise if they also opted for this possibly inauthentic means. A bigger part of me believes we were just glad to help others. We were not competing after all.

On the Camino it was important to move at one's own pace. *Refugio* health posters counseled people to find their own best rate for walking and not to try matching others. I took this to mean that I need not feel pressured to keep up with those who steamed ahead or to slow down for people who lagged behind. Pilgrims who traveled together sometimes spread out along the way as they went. They did not need to be side-by-side every moment all day long. Some managed better with sprinting. Others liked to plod an hour or two, rest for a time, and then proceed another hour or two. By evening, they were all together once more. The point wasn't to arrive ahead of anyone. Rather, one moved at one's own optimal and least taxing pace.

Assisting one another was an important aspect of this experience. I fondly remember pilgrims, some whose names I knew and others who remain anonymous, who gave advice about hostels and food, weather and conditions. When I got tendonitis toward the end of my journey, many freely offered counsel.

We all wanted and hoped for each person to succeed. In Santiago, at the journey's end, it was a pleasure worthy of celebration to recognize every person who arrived, no matter how long it took him or her to get there. This felt different than life as I normally live it.

NO ONE I'D RATHER BE WITH?

The Camino gave me good company, some of the best I've ever known, and I miss those folks.

Time and again, Camino veterans conclude the same thing about what is most special about this journey: the people. I was deeply moved by how we encountered and engaged one another.

Yet they were not necessarily companions I would select. Rather, I hung out with whoever was there at the time—on the trail, in the restaurant, at the hostel. I didn't inquire about religion or politics first. We administered no personality inventories to gauge relational compatibility. Rather, I savored the particular and peculiar gifts of each person.

This in itself was no small thing. It too was countercultural. These days we can be choosy about those to whom we relate and when. We plug into iPods or MP3s, distract ourselves with cell phones and ignore those around us. We e-mail or Blackberry anyone who seems more interesting, even if they are at some distance.

But I cannot help wonder what is lost. I once heard social philosopher Albert Borgmann remark that a way to recognize a particularly worthwhile moment is to be able to affirm: "There is no one I'd rather be with." Such a claim is far different than today's norms; our culture revolves around wanting to be elsewhere and desiring to pay attention to other people. I know stories of spouses who prefer e-mail over family, children who spend hours on Instant Messaging but do not converse at home, adults who choose deceptively anonymous cyber-relationships over messy, complicated, in-the-flesh versions.

The Camino reminded us that—to take liberties with an old rock song—if you can't be with the ones you prefer, then prefer the ones you're with.

¡BUEN CAMINO!

On a hilltop shortly after dawn we found one of the most famous and delightful spots on the Camino. The Monastery of Irache vineyard shared the bounty of its crops with passing pilgrims. I can still see Domingo there: a beefy, forty-something Spanish Marianist priest in improbable spandex biking shorts, grinning mischievously with plastic cup in hand, holding it aloft as if it was a priceless crystal chalice. (We had met a few days before while washing our clothes side by side in a *refugio* courtyard, quickly launching into a discussion of Teresa of Ávila and then moving into Christian perspectives on peace and justice issues.) This Irache respite was a rare moment of relaxation for him. His vacation only allowed him four weeks maximum to complete the journey, and so he generally walked fast and far every day. It was the last time that I saw him.

Along the way there were many water fountains for pilgrims, but Irache took hospitality further. Their fountain, the best known of the entire route, was inset into an external stone wall. The steel plate behind the taps bore an impressive coat of arms, the monastery's seal. All passersby were invited to stop and draw a cup of wine to hearten themselves for the journey—*con fuerza y vitalidad*—"with strength and vitality," as the welcoming sign invited. (There was also a water fountain there for those who chose not to indulge in fermented fruit of the vine.)

It was striking to see how this small gesture brought grins and laughter to pilgrims clustered there. We often discussed this fountain for the next four hundred miles, until the very end of my journey in fact. A small but generous act bore fruit long after the brief cheeriness of the wine itself. What was it that Jesus said about the eternal rewards of a small, cold cup given in hospitality?

Far simpler gestures meant much too. When pilgrims passed each other or said goodbye, they wished one another *¡Buen Camino!* (Spanish for "good way" or "good route"). Uncomplicated words of encouragement.

Pilgrims on bicycles regularly overtook us. I had heard that there could be tension between hikers and bikers, but I did not experience this. In fact, I was gratified that almost every single bicyclist cheerily called out *¡Buen Camino!* as he or she passed.

This short phrase was powerful. In one restaurant a waiter seemed surly. Because I was in a different culture, I could not always tell what was going on. So I did not make too much of his moodiness. But as I left, he wished me *¡Buen Camino!* Suddenly the way I felt about him and the meal of *paella* he had served me was completely changed. An ambiguous experience was sweetened.

Why not encourage every believer we meet with a blessing? Is it so hard to find a simple phrase to inspire others on the path, in their following of Jesus the Way, the true Camino?

And why only other believers? What could we offer everyone we encounter? Can we not commend them to God without sounding self-righteously pushy?

Philo of Alexandria, an ancient Jewish philosopher, is reputed to have said, "Be compassionate, for everyone you meet is fighting a great battle." This is invaluable counsel in ministry. It gives one patience and helps one listen. I use it when teaching about dealing with conflict and difficult behavior. How can we maintain such a mindset? On the Camino, as matters grew harder and our energy depleted, people became more inclined to help one another. As conditions worsened, compassion increased as well. We were all fighting a great battle, taking on a huge challenge, but we reminded each other that none of us was alone.

Most of us live privately and individualistically, isolated and cut off from one another. Instead of front porches for visiting with neighbors and passersby, our backyard decks are sheltered behind privacy fences. We no longer stroll on sidewalks, with opportunity to chat with pedestrians, homeowners and shopkeepers; rather cars move directly into and out of garages with automatic doors. As we drive, we keep windows closed; all the better to enjoy heat or air conditioning, music, or cell phone diversion. In the meantime we grow impatient with folks who drive slowly or hesitate a second too long at stoplights. Then we do not wish a *¡Buen Camino!* but honk horns or display certain fingers instead. No doubt many of us face challenges, but often we're not aware of what others undergo, with no sense of appreciation for their great struggles.

Growing up, I heard many stories from my parents about living through the Nazi occupation of their country. They were astonished by the level of cooperation in the resistance between Dutch Christians of various denominations. A few years earlier, folks of different traditions did not socialize, date or talk with one another. Now they risked their lives together. No doubt that World War II experience in Europe, the largest challenge most of them ever faced, a great battle indeed, contributed to the impressive ecumenical advances of the second half of the twentieth century.

Joining together before common obstacles can take the focus off matters that might otherwise divide. With all that threatens our world today—devastating wars, looming ecological catastrophes, astonishing poverty, disease epidemics—our era is no less demanding than that of previous generations. We all face immense challenges.

If small things—a shared bowl of *pulpo*, informal and affectionate address, a cup of wine, an encouraging phrase—make such a difference for pilgrims, what monumental things could be accomplished in the twenty-first century if Christians found simple ways to greet, encourage and honor their neighbors?

9

—

SECULAR SEEKERS

The Disconnect of Pilgrims and Church

—

Happy are the people whose strength is in you!
whose hearts are set on the pilgrims' way.

PSALM 84:4 BCP

DISAPPOINTED EXPECTATIONS AND RICH ENCOUNTERS

Felix, a devout Dutch Catholic, planned his pilgrimage itinerary so that he could attend mass each night wherever he happened to stay. But in Los Arcos this did not work, so he read the day's Gospel that evening by himself. Sitting outside, he pondered the Cana story of Jesus turning water into wine.

During this informal *lectio divina*, he longed for a cup of that particular beverage. Unbeknownst to him, nearby pilgrims were sharing wine at that time. Right then, they called and invited Felix to join them! It was not a Jesus-scale miracle—not even a miracle at all—but he found it moving and providential nonetheless. He explained this to his companions. Two listeners, raised in Eastern Europe, did not understand; they had never heard about water into wine.

In fact, many pilgrims were unchurched. A great number did not consider themselves even nominal Christians. At the end of the pilgrimage a young fellow who said he was not religious nevertheless told me he was surprised that so few pilgrims called themselves believers. He reported being immensely disappointed that pilgrims did not sing Christian songs together. Before the trip he anticipated vigorous group discussions on faith, God and the meaning of life. But that seldom happened for him, and he was sad about that. When theological matters were mentioned in conversations, he always and immediately went on high alert.

Some shied from discussing faith. We walked for a couple of hours early one morning with a young Swedish woman, Nila (who spoke excellent English with a pronounced and anomalous Australian accent). We did not know her well. She traveled for a week with a close-knit group of several nationalities: French, Spanish and Canadian. We saw them everywhere together. She intriguingly commented to us about two of her companions: "I think they must be quite devout, because they insist on going into every church that is open along the way." Yet in all their long conversations, never once did she know for sure.

My experience was different. People often asked me directly whether I was there for religious or spiritual motivations, or some other reason. (On the Camino, *religious* means Christian purposes of prayer or repentance, while *spiritual* indicates something more than secular goals but not necessarily Christian ones.) I was "religious," although few of my questioners were in that category. When people learned I was a seminary professor and ordained minister, many wanted to talk about faith matters.

A daughter of a former priest and former nun probed me on church history. "I'm very interested in the Templars," she exclaimed. A young navy veteran from Canada inquired about what the Scripture says regarding eternal consequences for unbelievers. A woman who was alienated from her formerly active church life—for reasons that were never clear to me—wanted to explore whether Jesus being the Son of God is unique to him. "We are all God too," she contended. An evangelical from the United States asked me to explain Catholic doctrines of transubstantiation; he was especially interested as he has Catholic in-laws. And a lapsed Spanish Catholic questioned me on the idea of Christian nonviolence, a notion that was unfamiliar and even perplexing to her.

I remember other times in my life when I related immediately and intensely with strangers on questions of faith and faithfulness. But those were usually explicitly Christian contexts such as Taizé or Daybreak, the L'Arche community where Henri Nouwen lived his last decade.

It was not only my vocation that led to such conversations on the Camino. On numerous occasions people quickly began a deep dialogue before names were even exchanged, let alone each other's occupation or core beliefs. (Eventually pilgrims usually exchanged first names, but in most cases I never heard surnames.) Within minutes of conversing over coffee at an outdoor café in Mansilla de las Mulas, someone who did not consider himself a Christian—and who knew virtually nothing about me, just my name and where I lived—began quizzing me about the meaning of the Sermon on the Mount! Happily, this is a favorite Mennonite text.

I too would have been enriched by more corporate singing and vigorous group conversations, yet the dialogues I had were a privilege that deepened the quality of my pilgrimage.

MIXED MOTIVES

We pilgrims had much in common, but were also a varied lot. We were young and old; I met teenagers, eighty-year-olds and all ages in between. One pilgrim was visibly pregnant; she literally carried a child with her. We were working class and professional. We came from Europe, Asia, Australia, North, South and Central America. We were also all over the map in terms of faith commitments. And pilgrims walked the Camino for many different motives.

A few devout Catholics were there in a full spirit of pilgrimage. But most Catholics told me that they did not "practice." One Frenchman, François, said he was just a "little bit Catholic." I also encountered Protestants, although they were far fewer in number.

Many walkers appeared to be emphatically not religious or spiritual. I had the impression that some were just there for the physical challenge, others for an economical vacation and still others because this was a great way to trek by foot. The Camino is for many Europeans what the Appalachian Trail is to Americans, an ultimate hiking experience.

I was a pastor long enough to know that people go to church for all kinds of reasons, not always for what one might regard as noble, edifying ones. This often shocks idealistic ministers fresh out of seminary. Some congregants attend because they've always done so. Others capitulate to family pressure. Some find it a good place to meet members of the opposite gender. A few, bored and lonely, look for something to do or somewhere to go. I was always glad for the many—if not most—who came out of deep Christian motivations, but also had to suspend my high expectations and trust God's ability to work in all circumstances.

I suspect that many were not even sure why they were on this path. They had difficulty naming reasons. They did not understand what drew them to this unique route.

Even so, people vigorously debated what it meant to be "authentic" pilgrims. Religious faith seldom entered such qualifications. Other factors did rate however. Those staying in *refugios* were more credible than those in hotels. Carrying one's pack was superior to having vehicles do it for you. Stefano, a chef from Italy, began by bike but decided that walking was preferable. So he put his bicycle in storage and continued on foot.

In the last week many begrudged those who journeyed only the final sixty miles. (The Cathedral grants a much-cherished Compostela certificate for going at least that minimal distance; most pilgrims covet that document.) Part of it, no doubt, had to do with some pride about our own costly achievement. When I lined up in the Cathedral office in Santiago for my Compostela, I was self-righteously unimpressed with those complaining of the difficulty of walking sixty miles. That was only four days after all. I resembled those resentful workers in Jesus' parable (Matthew 20:1-16) who begin working early in the day and begrudge latecomers receiving the same payment. But there was also the practical annoyance that the swelling numbers of newcomers made it more difficult to find places to stay that final week. (One companion proposed with inflamed passion that long-distance walkers should always be given preference in *refugios*.)

Authentic or inauthentic, mixed motives neither surprised nor disturbed me. Just read Chaucer's *Canterbury Tales* to see that pilgrims were always a varied lot. In medieval times, church and state authorities were aware that not all sojourners were saintly. Some went as a convenient way to get out of home responsibilities, avoid legal consequences of their deeds or escape debts. Others journeyed because it was a good means to exploit and profit from wayfarers. The church tried to regulate matters by demanding that pilgrims carry an authorizing credential from their home parish. (Now people are required to obtain a "pilgrim's passport" through a pilgrim's organization when they begin their journey. This document must be stamped every day in order for one to be eligible to stay in hostels and to receive the official Compostela certificate at the journey's end.) Mixed lot or not, I paid my companions more and more respectful attention as the journey progressed and found that we had much in common.

In Jesus' wheat and tares parable (Matthew 13:24-30), an enemy plants weeds alongside good seeds in a farmer's field. The owner opts not to remove invasive plants because that might "uproot the wheat along with them." Jesus recommended letting everything bide a while to see what might happen. This was good to remember while underway.

KEEPING COMPANY WITH THE OTHER

One of my most striking memories of the Camino is a sense of perpetual thirst. I consumed huge quantities of water each day. Once I purchased a two-quart bottle of lemon Fanta soda and proceeded to down it as I walked a shadeless path for the next several hours. I was even thirsty all night long. I took my bottle of water to bed with me and gulped it whenever I awoke. I was always parched. Thirst is a vivid scriptural image of our longing for God.

> O God, you are my God; eagerly I seek you;
>> my soul thirsts for you, my flesh faints for you,
>> as in a barren and dry land where there is no water.
> (Psalm 63:1 BCP)

Think of Jesus meeting the woman at the well and promising her: "those who drink of the water that I will give them will never be thirsty. The water that I will give will become in them a spring of water gushing up to eternal life" (John 4:14). My unremitting longing for water along the way reminds me how many pilgrims I met who were looking for God.

I had read and heard enough about the Camino ahead of time to anticipate traces of New Age emphases among some hosts and pilgrims. In the first two weeks I noticed little, even though I watched for it. As time passed, though, I heard more such ideas. For this Christian, rooted as I am in historical traditions and doctrines, such notions are unsettling. Yet I gradually found myself responding to "spiritual but not religious" pilgrims with more and more attention and compassion.

An overworked cliché speaks of the need to "walk a mile" in the shoes or moccasins of another to achieve deep understanding. Here we were walking far more than a mile together, and solidarity can be converting. That simple and respectful companionship with others got me to listen. Meals, rest stops and walking provided opportunity for long, leisurely conversation. There was no hurry to get things resolved; we had plenty of time to explore. As a professor—and formerly a preacher—I spend much time proclaiming the right way to think or theologize, but here I was called into a different, more attentive mode.

I had a chance to see folks as complex and authentic human beings, true neighbors and fellow strugglers, not some stereotype that is easy for me to dismiss. They too, as Philo of Alexandria's counsel reminds us, were fighting their own great battles.

As I reread the book of Acts, I see that the apostle Paul was brilliantly able to affirm the legitimate seeking even of idolaters!

> Then Paul stood in front of the Areopagus and said, "Athenians, I see how extremely religious you are in every way. For as I went through the city and looked carefully at the objects of your worship, I found among them an altar with the inscription, 'To an unknown god.' What therefore you worship as unknown, this I proclaim to you." (Acts 17:22-23)

Are we able to name what is worthwhile about questers in our time and tap into their longings to point them to Christ the Way?

I found many pilgrims to be people of reflection and virtue. Never before have I run into such an abundance of journalers! Each evening, folks wrote long entries in their notebooks. People I met wanted to live in ways that contributed to the well-being of others. They were unwilling to settle for selfish materialism or consumerism. They were convinced that there is "something more," that matters of the spirit are vital. I often experienced compassion and care: in hospitality, shared meals, companionship and concern for my well-being. Folks freely shared counsel and food, water and support.

Folks felt strongly about considering themselves pilgrims, *authentic* ones at that. They were comfortable on this route of Christian significance. They reveled in church art, architecture, history, rituals and symbols. Many visited each church building that was open, attended Mass whenever it was available and appreciated the pilgrims' blessings that were occasionally offered by local priests as we passed through their towns. Yet they also complained of the institutional church: its wealth and power, dogma and hypocrisy. Sadly, almost to a person, they were disbelieving when I talked about Christian nonviolence, a central idea for Mennonites; for people I met, the militarism of George W. Bush is now the face of Christianity. Some—without professing Christian faith—carried Bibles. And most seemed passionate about admiring Jesus. I came to understand that the best way to talk about my faith was to speak of following Jesus, certainly a good metaphor for any pilgrimage.

Unmoored from the church, some preferred conspiracy theories. There was fierce interest in Templars and *The DaVinci Code* (a bestseller in Spain too, alas). Some folks seemed credulous at times with their potpourri of ideas about reincarnation, auras, harmonic convergence, crystals, energy and karma. Still, these were seekers who thirsted and longed for God. I ruefully recognized that I had paid insufficient attention to such folks before, not just on the Camino.

I am not alone. The church as a whole is often largely absent to such folks. This was vividly illustrated on the Camino when people lamented that so few churches were open. Many pilgrims wanted to visit.

Yet most buildings were locked, and the few that were not often felt more like museums than places of prayer and worship, sometimes even charging entrance fees!

There were happy—but all too rare—exceptions. About forty-five miles before Santiago, Agape Campus, an evangelical student network based in Spanish universities, has an outreach ministry to pilgrims in the village of Ligonde. Their *Fuente del Peregrino* (pilgrim's fountain) offers water and coffee to passersby, as well as literature, including Bibles and pilgrimage psalms. Best of all, I found the volunteer staff are glad to interact with pilgrims. One of my companions, a young university student with many questions, stayed behind and conversed with a volunteer there for over an hour. Later, he debriefed with me about what he heard.

On the whole there is a larger missed opportunity. Is there not a way for the church—not just along the Camino but elsewhere as well—to welcome such seekers? Can we not respond to this yearning with hospitable listening and conversation? On the Camino many pilgrims asked themselves the most basic and most important questions: Who am I? What is the purpose of life? Am I significant? Is how I behave important? How ought I to live? Is there reason for hope? These are existential matters, the very concerns that Christians profess to know something about.

The Taizé community in France could be a good model: deeply rooted in historical Christian faith, it extends a hospitable and listening presence to seekers from around the world. (See appendix three for info about Taizé.) I remember my intense weeklong visit there in the summer of 2000, along with 4,500 other pilgrims representing over sixty nations. The worship, Bible studies and meals all provided a setting for safe exploration and gentle proclamation of the gospel.

Shortly before returning to the United States, I met up with Féliz, someone I had encountered a few times in the previous two weeks. Skinny and small, this thirty-year-old stood out in any crowd of pilgrims. His thick dark hair was matted into long black dreadlocks. And he never changed his clothes. His garb was simple, a T-shirt and frayed jeans that he cut off very short, so that most of his legs were visible. He was quiet, but one evening I saw a *hospitalero* harass him over petty regulations. Here, at the end of his journey, Féliz was suffering. He had a large and nasty, ulcerated sore on his foot, and he was hobbling. But his spirits were in worse shape. He had been treated so rudely in the Cathedral office, that he'd decided to burn his Compostela, the certificate so many of us wanted and cherished. The officials there had quizzed him relentlessly, not believing he had actually walked that entire route. Not having been there with him in that office, it's impossible for me to understand exactly what happened or whether he contributed to the problem. But I know that I was not interrogated when I was in that office, saw that happen to no one else and suspect that Féliz may have received that treatment because of his countercultural appearance. If so, this was an injustice, one that symbolizes for me how often the church (and that includes me) gets things wrong.

If the church focused less on institutional power, protection and self-interest, and more on prayer, mysticism and the spiritual life, we might still have an opportunity to be heard. As I became acquainted with various pilgrims and we helped one another, I found that conversion went two ways and that I too was being called to new convictions.

PILGRIMAGE VERSUS CHURCH-GOING

People often told me they were "spiritual but not religious." They believed in God, matters of the spirit or at least "something more," but wanted to do so in a way that was divorced from the burdens and constraints of religious dogma and institutions and all their tawdry history. (Ironically, we evangelicals bear some responsibility for this iffy and questionable distinction. When I was a teen, we casually and self-righteously called Christians like ourselves "spiritual," while dismissing others as "fleshly" or merely "religious.")

I was not entirely surprised by these implicit tensions between pilgrims and institutions even on the Camino itself. Pilgrimages are by their very nature often anarchic and theologically subversive. As early as the ninth century the church warned against false pilgrims, whose ranks included folks avoiding household responsibilities, others looking for adventures and illicit romance, thieves, women of ill repute and beggars. I did not meet such a colorful array myself. In medieval times pilgrim routes were also often the base for heretical evangelism. Galicia, the region where Santiago is located, was in the thirteenth and fourteenth centuries a hub of heretical speculation. Actually, Galicia was known as the source of heresies as early as the fourth century. That may still be the case!

Nevertheless, it seemed odd that so many non-Christians ventured on that route now. Those medieval pilgrims—even heretical ones—at least went under Christian guise. But now on the Camino people rejecting Christianity and the church were walking a pilgrimage path.

Curiously, pilgrimages might be increasing. Some argue that this form of devotion rises as church-going diminishes. In Europe church attendance is low and steadily dwindling; even so, the Camino attracts tens of thousands each year. Western Europe now has over six thousand pilgrimage sites drawing as many as 100 million people a year.

Are there clues here to how the church might respond to this pilgrim hunger? We need to listen to such folks, even those who do not fit our tidy theological categories.

Originally, most Christian pilgrimage sites and routes were popularly initiated. They were not begun by church leaders or hierarchies.

Local folks in one place would venerate one of their own—a martyr, mystic or miracle worker—as a saint, and others began coming to pay homage. Or a lay person would have a vision or divine encounter, and people visited to be in touch with that manifestation. The wider church and its hierarchies generally got into the act of these pilgrimages only after they were well underway. Then church leaders tried to channel that energy for their own purposes. The church could pay attention again to newly emerging forms of pilgrimage.

Along the way I wished for companions who journeyed in the spirit of Taizé. Imagine a small group of pilgrims committed to a simple, shared discipline of prayer and praise. They would walk the Camino, as that is the best way to encounter other pilgrims and to be regarded as authentic as well. They would listen to other travelers. And they would share their faith perspectives when appropriate.

When I was in Britain in 2000, church folk were still trying to make sense of the spontaneous responses to Princess Diana's death three years earlier. I interviewed an Anglican priest, Ray Simpson, who told me, "It was the most extraordinary event of public ritual in my life." He quoted a prominent bishop: "The people out there are not where we thought. They are very interested in the spiritual, but we haven't connected." Simpson sadly concluded that church "worship has generally lost its street credibility."

A Camino pilgrim I met actively sponsors rave parties in Australia that involve neither drugs nor alcohol. He was seminary trained, although he no longer considers himself Christian. (He once was active in church, he told me, but several issues came to a head for him. So on one Sunday, he stood up from where he was playing guitar during worship and walked straight out of the sanctuary, never to return.) An important aspect of his work now in Australia is the sponsoring of life rituals for people who are not part of a religious institution. He clearly regards this as a secular form of ministry, a new and much-needed kind of pastoral care.

Do we offer worship services and other opportunities for prayer that might be hospitable for folks who do not regularly attend church? In an era when North Americans work longer hours than four decades ago and perpetually complain of being busy, can we provide space for sabbath and rest, renewal and reorientation? Think of the impressive success of the Methodist Walk to Emmaus movement, retreats of prayer and worship that have by now involved thousands of participants; I wonder whether the church might not offer retreats geared for seekers too.

The last church I served as pastor was located in the country. Because of its isolation, it always kept its doors locked. Yet I know that occasionally people—not necessarily church attenders—would come to pray. They had to content themselves with staying in the parking lot or venturing into the cemetery. Now, of course, it is common for churches—even in well-trafficked areas—to be closed to casual visitors during the week. But we raise the threshold against inquirers if we only permit or expect them to show up on Sunday mornings for formal services.

And what if churches took the simple act of walking seriously once more, that preeminent and basic pilgrim mode of movement? I lament the fact that most people in our society who attend church do so by driving. I know some need to take cars for various reasons, but I wish they were the exception rather than the norm. In the nineteenth century, nature lover John Burroughs grew concerned that people were forgoing the pleasures of walking to church and choosing rather to ride animals and wagons. He wished to see Christians on foot.

I think I should be tempted to go to church myself if I saw all my neighbors starting off across the fields or along paths that led to such charmed spots, and were sure I should not be jostled or run over by the rival chariots of the worshipers at the temple doors. I think that is what ails our religion; humility and devoutness of heart leave one when he lays by his walking shoes and walking clothes, and sets out for church drawn by something.

Indeed, I think it would be tantamount to an astonishing revival of religion if the people would all walk to church on Sunday and walk home again. . . . They would walk away from their *ennui*, their worldly cares, their uncharitableness, their pride of dress; for these devils always want to ride, while the simple virtues are never so happy as when on foot.

If the church took pilgrimage lessons more seriously, we might yet connect with people of good faith who still want and long to meet God. Their hearts, as Augustine taught us, are also restless. We could learn again from pilgrims. We'd be in good company. Jesus often journeyed with people on the move. It was there that he taught followers, encountering and evangelizing newcomers. There he listened to questions and concerns. There he observed how people lived and what preoccupied them. The road was where he was usually found, and it was his classroom, podium, laboratory and sanctuary.

It could be ours as well.

10

—

FOCAL WAYS OF LIFE

Putting Pilgrimage into Practice

—

Show me your ways, O LORD,
and teach me your paths.
Lead me in your truth and teach me,
for you are the God of my salvation;
in you have I trusted all the day long.

PSALM 25:3-4 BCP

PILGRIMAGE AND RESTLESSNESS

Before my sojourn I spoke often with many acquaintances about my plans. Frequently, friends had never heard of the Camino. I tried comparing it to the Appalachian Trail, but some were unaware of that too. I realized that places that most engage me and loom large in my imagination are off the radar screens for many. Yet pilgrimage remains relevant.

Even secular people have sacred sites, ones often important to Christians too. Many find reason to go to the Lorraine Motel in Memphis where Martin Luther King Jr. was assassinated, the Vietnam Memorial in Washington, D.C., Wounded Knee in South Dakota, Ground Zero in Manhattan, the Anne Frank House in Amsterdam, Hiroshima and Nagasaki in Japan. I understand and appreciate the merit of such locations; I have visited most of them, and those I have not yet seen I still hope to encounter someday.

But not everything that may resemble pilgrimage is necessarily hallowed.

North American culture is highly mobile. I myself have moved way too often, and I am not alone. I like to think I answered God's call in those transitions, but I suspect that I also did so because of career opportunities, if not advancement. I am challenged in this regard by a fellow resident of Indiana, essayist Scott Russell Sanders, to take more seriously the merit of "staying put." Our unsettled way of life detracts from our ability to honor any place. If we do not learn how to detect God standing still, we'll not find God when we're moving around either. Thus one of three central Benedictine vows is stability, the promise to remain committed to a single place and its community for the rest of one's life, trusting that God will speak and convert even—and perhaps especially—when that place no longer easily entertains. Once, I was struggling in my work as a pastor and felt tempted to find easier work without the complications of congregational life. Henri Nouwen encouraged me to stay instead and, in his words, "go deeper."

North American mobility is all part of a bigger picture, I suspect. And our moving around does not appear to satisfy us. There are obviously serious things awry in our lives. We are frantic, frenetic and frazzled. People sleep less and work more. Too many acquaintances I care about are addicted to computer games or Internet pornography. Families eat together less and less. Folks gobble down food on the run. Churches have difficulty scheduling the simplest, most basic events. I do not rest easy with how I live my life. And I suspect that our culture's steadily increasing interest in spirituality has a lot to do with the fact that many of us function in ways that are personally and ecologically unsustainable.

FOCAL LIVING

Wilderness author Sigurd Olson wrote these insightful words a half century ago:

> There is a restlessness within us, an impatience with things as they are, which modern life with its comforts and distractions does not seem to satisfy. We sense intuitively that there must be something more, search for panaceas we hope will give us a sense of reality, fill our days and nights with such activity and our minds with such busyness that there is little time to think. When the pace stops we are often lost, and we plunge once more into the maelstrom hoping that if we move fast enough, somehow we may fill the void within us. We may not know exactly what it is we are listening for, but we hunt as instinctively . . . as sick animals look for healing herbs.

Olson put his finger on something awry with our way of life today, and we need help with such questions. One place the church can engage the spiritual longing in our culture is to name the shallowness of how many of us live and to offer and model more grace-filled approaches. I am particularly taken with the wisdom of Albert Borgmann, a social philosopher who is deeply informed by Christian faith, in his analysis of how contemporary culture—with its emphasis on technology and consumerism—forms us, our characters, our families, our friendships and most important relationships. In fact, he would argue that the forces of technology and consumerism too often deeply deform us. He holds out alternative ways of living, favoring a lifestyle he names as "focal."

Focal living helps us identify and perceive Olson's "something more," a quality of life that we miss and long to find. Focal living poses a telling contrast to the many aspects of our reality today that "lead to a disconnected, disembodied, and disoriented sort of life." When existence seems shallow and unfulfilling, focal concerns can "center and illuminate our lives." That sounds lovely and inviting, but how do we recognize such priorities?

Focal concerns are objects, activities or practices with several qualities.

First they have a "commanding presence." They take energy or effort; they make demands on us. They require discipline, attention and focus. And they are beyond our control and beyond our ability to manipulate or consume. When I hike, I take up a focal practice. It may be strenuous, but it also engages me with focal objects (forests, wilderness, mountains). Preparing a meal is a focal practice that requires the discipline of working with food. A commanding presence involves effort, skills, patience and persistence.

Second, focal things and practices have deep and evident connections with the wider world, including people and our ecosystem. Playing a musical instrument links one with the artisan who created it, the composer whose music one plays, musical traditions one honors, musicians who join in and friends or audiences who listen. Gardening puts us in touch with the earth but also with food, farmers and those who eat our produce. When my spouse bakes a loaf of bread there are all kinds of lively connections; but when I thaw a frozen microwave dinner I am in no explicit relationship with anyone.

Third, focal realities have "centering" or orienting power. They help us experience and be in touch with something "as greater than myself and of ultimate significance." Decades ago, I traveled to Paris as a young adult. I was a convinced Anabaptist sectarian who doubted the worth or merit of many Christian traditions, especially Catholicism. And I was not in the least interested in architecture. But my first day in that city I happened to pass the Cathedral of Notre Dame and decided to drop in for a visit. I was not in pilgrimage mode, but it was a "must-see" tourist site after all. From the first moment I entered the doors, I was dumbfounded. I shocked myself by exclaiming almost aloud: "Oh . . . I want to be a Catholic!" I realized that here was an overwhelming tradition that had much to teach me, and I savored the beauty before me. Perhaps I was on a pilgrimage after all. Cathedrals are focal things, as are museums, works of art, trees, wilderness areas and quilts.

Focal things move, teach, inspire and reassure. "Focal reality gathers and illuminates our world." Each of us could compile our own lists. Focal practices include athletic endeavors, artistry, poetry, reading, gardening, writing, hospitality, cooking, flower-arranging, meaningful work, music and on and on. Just so focal things: arts, crafts, pottery, tapestries, museums and churches. These concerns are abundantly available, and what each of us names in our own lists says as much about us as it does about our surroundings and circumstances. These aspects—commanding presence, continuity and centering power—pose possibilities counter to the many factors today that diminish the quality of our lives. But we need not settle for such depletion and diminishment. One reason the Camino is so attractive is that it points to different ways and possibilities for living.

In a revealing moment, Borgmann talked at a consultation I attended in 2001 of an important turning point in his life. As a young adult living in Germany decades ago, he had been facing many difficulties and found it hard to keep perspective. Right around then he was directed in a retreat by the renowned theologian Hans Urs von Balth-asar. Von Balthasar tried to uncover—and help Borgmann recognize—whether there were moments of God's grace even in that challenging time. There Borgmann discovered something he often uses with students.

I tell them about the four focal affirmations and ask them,
"When were you last able to affirm them?"
There is no place I would rather be.
There is nothing I would rather do.
There is no one I would rather be with.
This I will remember well.

The Camino was in every sense a focal place, and my walking of it a focal experience. There I could often embrace Borgmann's four affirmations. And the pilgrimage nudged me to consider how I might live more focally as well. No surprise then that so many of us pilgrims on that route reevaluated our lifestyles.

This pilgrimage repeatedly offered glimpses of what life could be like but all too seldom is. It gave peeks at kingdom possibilities. Yet it is hard to honor such priorities. Too quickly my life gets caught up in stress and striving, busyness and preoccupation, competition and achievement. Another way of life, a more redemptive vision, is available. It is there; it needs to be embraced. We no more have to invent it from scratch than we need to create the Camino ourselves. But we do have to reach out deliberately and embrace focal living. That persistent kind of determination can be surprisingly difficult, especially when too few around us are stretching themselves in similar directions. Yet both Borgmann and the Camino convincingly demonstrate why such efforts are ultimately worthwhile.

While "focal" terminology was not actually part of the vocabulary of pilgrims I met, I suspect that the focal reality we experienced was a factor that drew them to this path. My evidence for that has to do with the quality of relationships pilgrims experienced along the way and the depths of reflections sparked by such encounters. On the Camino we caught a glimpse of life-giving possibilities.

Good Company

Pilgrims walked the Camino in various ways.

Many went alone. (In fact, a lot of solo pilgrims were women, and they reported to me that they always felt safe.) Some connected with other travelers early in the journey and stuck together for the rest of the route. Some walked in prearranged groups. In one small and cozy *refugio*, an older weather-beaten woman wandered around casting an occasional Dutch phrase left and right. She was nevertheless surprised when I responded in Dutch. She had turned sixty-five the previous spring and celebrated her retirement and pension by setting out with a longstanding friend by foot from Amsterdam on Easter Sunday. They walked over two months together, but suddenly in Spain her companion decided she needed solitude. As we visited together, I heard someone who was struggling with unanticipated loneliness. I never learned her name and never saw her again.

Many covered the five hundred miles in one stretch, as I did. (A few walked two or even three or more times that far.) But others could not get such a block of time free and came back year after year for one or two week stints. They were deeply dedicated to this project, often planning and pursuing it for years.

As we progressed on the Camino, a few dropped away. Several did so because they had to return for work (as was the case with my wife). Along the route others would join, folks beginning at a later point. Until the last sixty miles, pilgrims kept arriving. In spite of the variety of means and circumstances, there was a strong sense of togetherness. We were all on the Camino and going a similar direction. We all had something unusual in common.

I marveled at how well things worked and what a good job folks did at cooperating. I've been on many retreats and know how wonderful it is when people get along in such settings. Of course, on a short-term basis this is not necessarily so hard; there are things one can tolerate and overlook for a few days.

Retreats can be a rarefied space, but idealistic intentions might be hard to uphold during the long haul. Over the years I have lived often with fellow believers in households and know that no matter how spiritual or Christian they or I may be, getting along is hard work. Matters do not always proceed as smoothly as we might idealistically hope. Well-meaning saints or not, sometimes we still had trouble keeping the toilet paper supplied.

Yet among the Camino pilgrims I seldom saw a serious disagreement. There were occasional annoyances and irritations, to be sure, but my overall experience was positive. And I, you must understand, am normally a pessimist! As we learned to cope with the bigger challenges of this long-distance walking, small aggravations we might feel with one another seemed puny and petty.

Such success cannot be taken for granted. The intense pilgrim life had plenty of potential for conflict and problems. We shared close space every night. Often there was only one toilet or shower for dozens of people. Every day most of us did our wash by hand. In a seedy hostel there was but one laundry tub for over a hundred people to use; that line got long and tested tempers.

A lot of people passed through these hostels, often thousands per month. It was hard to keep them well-maintained and clean. I occasionally found it difficult to relax in settings that were not as hygienic as I would prefer. While we were careful with possessions, it was impossible to keep everything safe and secure at all times. One could not take one's backpack into the shower and did not want to carry it to meals. So, important and even valuable items were simply left behind in the *refugios*. And there was no way to guard our goods while sleeping.

Travel can be stressful and taxing. I often—too often—fly on planes. There, movement is also cramped, crowded and uncomfortable; conditions are confined. Boundaries are vague and travelers bump up against and into one another. There, as well, we move in a common direction. Yet such travel feels qualitatively different. I am usually drained and enervated by the end of those air journeys. I avoid the eyes of others and am not particularly interested in making new acquaintances. But on the Camino I responded to fellow sojourners with openness and trust. I was eager to engage others, and I was vulnerable with them.

What was the secret to this collaboration?

Focus on shared commitment to an extraordinary goal united us. We were not rivals in a contest with each other. We were not in a marathon race to get to Santiago before others or even to the next hostel first. Rather, we were joined in a project that was difficult and challenging, perhaps even outrageous. We knew we needed each other. If the system broke down, we would all suffer and pay the price. Cooperation, rather than competition, made all the difference. And the secure embrace of such an unusual context also invited converting self-scrutiny.

WORTHY WORK

A persistent theme in Camino conversations was people's occupations. No doubt this was partly because a standard ice-breaking conversational gambit is the question, So what do you do for a living? It is a mostly reliable way to make small talk with strangers.

This inquiry was even more pertinent since it was easy to wonder how people had the time to undertake such a trip. (Many Europeans use annual vacations and walk a week or two at a stretch.) As a professor I was privileged to be able to attempt this pilgrimage in one go, but I was in awe at those who stepped all the way from Austria or the Netherlands, some people setting aside as much as six or more months.

Yet there was more going on than curiosity or making small talk about occupations that made inquiries about jobs vital. Careers can be places where we feel conflicted and torn. The Camino inevitably raised issues for many. On a grand scale we pondered "the meaning of life." We engaged questions about how we choose to live, where we expend time and energy, and how we employ gifts. One of life's most soul-killing choices is to work at variance with what we know to be true, good, just or beautiful.

And so as we walked, we talked. Not just about what we did for a living but how we felt about our occupations. I, for example, spoke of love for my job but my longing at the same time to feel less like a foreigner and to live once again in the land of my birth. I identify deeply with biblical metaphors about exile, but I do not always rest easy in that sensibility: "I have been an alien residing in a foreign land" (Exodus 2:22).

I encountered numerous folks who pondered transitions, especially in their careers and vocations. Some considered a different geographical or institutional location for their work. Others seriously looked at changing occupations altogether. Several found clarity in what they needed to do to make their labor more meaningful.

Three sets of issues surfaced again and again.

People often considered whether or not they led balanced lives. Were they working too much, too hard? Hisako, a surgeon from Japan, visited with me over a memorable and tasty supper of roasted red peppers and lightly grilled steak in the small hillside farming town of Ferreiros. She spoke of the impressive demands in her institutional setting and of her sadness that her intense work did not leave room for her love of the arts. She got in touch with me after I went home and explained that convictions that emerged on the Camino gave her courage to make changes in her employment.

Or pilgrims discussed whether their particular jobs were personally meaningful. Some complained that they were bureaucratic functionaries, putting in time or pushing paper. They felt diminished and unfulfilled.

Some wondered if their occupations contributed to wider well-being. They noted institutional or political pressures that kept them from providing services and using gifts in ways they felt called. Were they benefiting their neighbors?

These vocational struggles were reminders that work is intended by God to be more than just a means to an end, a way to put money in the bank and food on the table. People of faith can legitimately—and indeed must—wrestle with questions of pace and balance, meaning and fulfillment, contribution and making a difference. And this time apart helped us all to focus our questions and enter into unexpected discernment.

So it was no surprise that we often heard conversion stories of people whose lives got reoriented by the Camino and who gave themselves to caring for other pilgrims.

One woman we met walked the pilgrimage alone some years ago. As she approached a small isolated *refugio* in a remote valley, she heard someone there playing a flute and spontaneously decided to remain there, and has done so now for years! Her parents, I'm told, were not pleased. She ministers to the physical aches and pains of passing pilgrims and is appreciated for the hospitality she now offers.

A young thirtyish man I met never questioned his factory job but then took a month for the pilgrimage. He caught a vision on the route, quit his work and bought an old house in Castrojeriz. He is refurbishing that stone edifice as a place of hospitality for pilgrims. He was one of the most gracious *hospitaleros* I met.

Such accounts are almost beyond comprehension, except that they have a biblical ring to them. After all, the apostle James worked as a fisherman when Jesus came by: "Immediately [Jesus] called them; and they left their father Zebedee in the boat with the hired men, and followed him" (Mark 1:20). I pray that the convictions of such brave pilgrims will keep me examining my own tightly held values and misguided choices.

II

—

WALKING IN FAITH

Walking as Spiritual Practice

—

But those who wait for the LORD shall renew their strength,
they shall mount up with wings like eagles,
they shall run and not be weary,
they shall walk and not faint.

ISAIAH 40:31

HOW LOVELY ARE THE FEET

When the local newspaper did a story on my pilgrimage after I returned, it included a picture of my one badly blistered foot. That photo attracted as much commentary as anything else in the article. When I show slides of my journey, that particular picture always elicits strong visceral responses. People are caught off-guard by such glaring attention to a part of the body we often overlook or even hide. That picture sparked thousands of words.

Feet got a lot of attention on the Camino. I have not spoken as much about that part of my body in over four dozen years of life as I did in those thirty-one days. Pilgrims discussed muscle pains, tendonitis, socks and footwear. In the past I have not always fully appreciated my wife's eagerness to describe her latest experiences as an operating room nurse—especially not over dinner!—but on the Camino I and others keenly detailed our most recent physical symptoms. We often compared theories on blisters and their prevention and treatment. Nothing seemed guaranteed. Even experienced hikers Carole, Eléanor or Wendy—who had trekked Nepal, Mongolia and the Appalachian Trail—got them. It was not uncommon to comment on sprains, sores and even blister leakage while sharing a meal. One day an unlikely looking pilgrim, a twenty-something American woman who carried herself like a model, caught me off-guard by asking for counsel: "What do you recommend for treating an open wound where I accidentally tore off all my skin?"

In restaurants, pilgrims casually pulled off muddy shoes and smelly socks and matter-of-factly examined aching feet, while enjoying whatever food or drink that establishment offered. As I've said, rules were different on the Camino.

Somewhere along the way, our culture grew embarrassed about, perhaps even ashamed of, feet. When I went to pastor my last congregation, I could not understand why they were proud of being one of the first area churches to abandon a centuries-old Mennonite ritual of footwashing. I tried to reintroduce this sacrament but encountered resistance. The church I now attend still practices footwashing twice a year, but many members elect not to participate; they vote without their feet, as it were.

Compared to Bible times, our feet are pampered with better footwear and options of pedicures and by the fact that we hardly use them. (Statistics suggest that Americans walk just a few hundred yards a day, less than a mile and a half a week.) Perhaps we're ashamed of our feet because we do not put them to the good purpose for which they are intended.

On the Camino I grew increasingly aware of how much press feet get in the Bible. Think of the attention to their anointing. Or the footwashing that Jesus initiated. Because that culture was used to walking, often long distances in hot weather with relatively poor footwear, it is no surprise that this part of the body receives so much scriptural exposure.

I learned to treat my feet with lotion before, during and after hikes. I liked this. I felt as if I was anointing and honoring them. And they surely deserved it. They had worked hard and accomplished much. They were worthy of wonder. As Thich Nhat Hanh often observes: not only walking on water is a marvel, even walking on the earth is a miracle. Thank God, then, for feet!

A favorite verse in Isaiah reads:

> How beautiful upon the mountains
> are the feet of the messenger who announces peace,
> who brings good news,
> who announces salvation,
> who says to Zion, "Your God reigns." (Isaiah 52:7)

In fact, the Scriptures regard feet as an important metaphor for bringing and carrying the truth. It does not take much imagination to know that the feet of mountain travelers in the Isaiah passage were probably blistered and battered, smelly and sore, twisted and torn as well. And yet they were surely lovely indeed.

Jesus' feet merit much spotlighting in the Bible. In Luke 7 a sinful woman "stood behind him at his feet," then took an alabaster jar and proceeded to "bathe his feet with her tears and to dry them with her hair. Then she continued kissing his feet and anointing them with ointment" (v. 38). How often those appendages are mentioned in just a few verses. Elsewhere people fall at Jesus' feet (Luke 8:41). Mary, and others, "sat at the Lord's feet" (Luke 10:39). When Jesus is encountered after his resurrection, the two Marys "took hold of his feet, and worshiped him" (Matthew 28:9). And when Jesus proved that he was truly alive after the resurrection, he presented both his hands and his feet (Luke 24:39-40). Adoration, worship and honoring of Jesus often include and focus on his feet.

It is not just Jesus' or others' feet, of course, that get so much attention in the Bible, but more specifically their function. What they do—walking—is vital to Christian faithfulness.

WE'VE COME THIS FAR BY FEET

My belated interest in walking—which did not bloom until I was middle-aged—helped me see its importance in Scriptures. Until then, I had no idea that this was a major theme and metaphor there.

Walking is an essential human faculty. It is deeply connected to who and how we are, and to who and how God made us.

> Thus says God, the LORD,
>> who created the heavens and stretched them out,
>> who spread out the earth and what comes from it,
>> who gives breath to the people upon it
>> and spirit to those who walk in it (Isaiah 42:5).

This humble, elementary mode of exercise is related to having God's Spirit and being able to breathe; it is mentioned in the same poem as the lofty subject of God's creation of heaven and earth.

In the Scriptures, inability to walk, being lame, is one of the most basic impediments to living fully. This disadvantage is as serious as being blind, deaf or mute. Many miracles deal with helping people gain the full use of feet and legs. When John the Baptist is in prison and needs further clarity and confirmation, Jesus responds by asserting that one vital sign of his messiahship is that "the lame walk" (Matthew 11:5; Luke 7:22).

We know about the restorative and healing potential of moving by foot. Sometimes when someone is steamed or out of sorts, we advise them to take a walk, cool down, get perspective. Many folks report finding clarity on dilemmas while going for a stroll. I have no trouble believing an old Latin saying often attributed to Augustine: *Solvitur ambulando*—"It is solved by walking." In my life I associate walking with healing too. More than once this discipline carried and cured me in times of depression, anxiety, burnout and other crises. In recent years this practice reoriented me in prioritizing my life and trying to understand our culture.

This basic human faculty, then, is a metaphor for faithful living. This is intriguingly and evocatively suggested in passages that indicate God's accompanying us:

> As God said,
> "I will live in them and walk among them,
> and I will be their God,
> and they shall be my people" (2 Corinthians 6:16).

God's relationship with us originally involved ambling: "They heard the sound of the LORD God walking in the garden at the time of the evening breeze" (Genesis 3:8). Conversely, Scriptures mention people whose connection with God is so closely intimate that there is only one way to describe it: "Enoch walked with God" (Genesis 5:22); "Noah walked with God" (Genesis 6:9). Others walked "before" God (Genesis 24:40; 48:15). They lived and moved in God's presence and sight.

This language figuratively describes faithful living. It is associated with virtuous lifestyles: trust, freedom, righteousness, integrity, fearing God, truthfulness, an undivided heart, blamelessness, lawfulness, goodness, justice, understanding, humility and obedience. This mode of movement is intended to reflect God's purposes and our life with God. Repeatedly, idols are mocked and derided specifically for inability to stride or stroll. "They have . . . feet, but do not walk" (Psalm 115:7); "they have to be carried, for they cannot walk" (Jeremiah 10:5); idols "cannot see or hear or walk" (Revelation 9:20).

There are other noteworthy aspects of this scriptural metaphor. In English we know that metaphorical feet can go astray, with a foot in our mouth or even in the grave. Like all God's good gifts, symbolic rambling too can go awry and be twisted from its purposes. It is possible, Scriptures warn, to walk in darkness (Psalm 82:5; Proverbs 2:13; John 12:35; I John 1:6), blindness (Zephaniah 1:17), sinful practices (Colossians 3:5-7) or the flesh (2 Corinthians 10:3 KJV). The first verse of the Psalms counsels against those who step according to "the advice of the wicked" (Psalm 1:1). (We may not always notice such metaphorical language, depending on our translations. The New King James Version favors *walk*, while the New Revised Standard Version often employs other terms.) These are significant admonitions. But what is even more striking is the fact that wayward walking gets cited so infrequently, while many more Bible quotes remark on faithful footwork.

God promises we will be able to follow in fidelity in spite of obstacles, dangers and hazards. "Even though I walk through the darkest valley, I fear no evil" (Psalm 23:4). (I am old-fashioned enough to miss the stately King James Version "through the valley of the shadow of death.") Or consider: "Though I walk in the midst of trouble, you preserve me against the wrath of my enemies" (Psalm 138:7). A passage that I often used pastorally is: "when you walk through fire you shall not be burned, and the flame shall not consume you" (Isaiah 43:2).

God promises not only protection in faithfulness but also that we will be empowered; we will "run and not be weary, . . . walk and not faint" (Isaiah 40:31; see Proverbs 4:12). Those who "walk uprightly" will know rest and peace (Isaiah 57:2).

Over and again, choosing to follow God's priorities is couched in the language of hikers and other trekkers. We are offered the choice of living by God's purposes. "Obey my voice, and I will be your God, and you shall be my people; and walk only in the way that I command you, so that it may be well with you" (Jeremiah 7:23).

A startling aspect of Jesus' ministry to the lame is that he often did it with words alone. When he healed the Bethesda man in John 5, his counsel was simple: "Stand up, take your mat and walk" (v. 8). I wonder whether the man already had the faculty but did not know or claim it. Jesus called him to his true agency and ability.

Such counsel challenges us because clearly there is something amiss in how we live today. People these days complain of unprecedented busyness. These laments are not merely imaginary. We work more than ever; hours spent on our jobs have been growing steadily in recent decades. But does God intend for us to be constantly torn and tugged in different directions? Could it be that by trying to keep pace with a culture without speed limits we are out of step with the life that God longs for us to have?

Christ calls us as well to stand up and stride today: in faithfulness, in God's purposes, in God's light.

EXPANDING SPIRITUAL PRACTICES

After a year of teaching, I felt overwhelmed. It was not just the pressures of a new vocation but giving up my life as a pastor and the costly move my family made to enable my opportunity to teach. I was done in and depleted. So I hiked for six days on the Bruce Trail in Ontario.

On that journey I felt myself relax, the tensions streaming away. I decompressed from the strain of working intensely for months while dealing with an emotionally draining agenda. I grew more and more centered. I paid attention to beautiful surroundings. I heard familiar Scripture texts in fresh ways. I was clear about priorities each day. Suddenly I did not feel so torn by conflicting expectations.

This helped me reevaluate how I had lived the last months. I could see clearly—and without great anxiety—that many focal concerns (reading, writing, prayer, family) had not received their proper due for some time. I resolved to live differently, "to pay attention to the deepest thing [I] know," as Douglas Steere evocatively described prayer.

What particularly struck me was that this process resembled how I experience retreats, a practice important to me for decades. They are crucial to my mental and spiritual health. I dare not live without them. Occasionally, when too long passes between retreats, my family reminds me of my need sooner than I am aware. I grow difficult to live with, and they helpfully suggest, "Isn't it time you visit the monastery again?" During such excursions I can predict themes that invariably arise.

First, I relax, start to breathe deeply and slowly release tensions and stresses. Next, I examine carefully what most pressured or bothered me recently. I gain helpful perspectives now that I am at a distance and no longer in the midst of things. Then, I see how my life started to get out of balance and out of whack. (Sadly, I confess that I've faced the same faults within myself for decades.) Finally, I get clarity about where to address the latest situations in my life that need recentering. I go home with new resolve that will carry me for some time, although I eventually and inevitably need another retreat.

While hiking had a similar effect as "more spiritual" retreats, it had other benefits worth noting. One is, of course, the physical value of exercise. As mentioned before, I suspect that walking stimulated both hemispheres of my brain and enhanced reflection. Another is the joy of encountering God's good earth so directly.

Hiking also led me to ponder something else. At seminary I occasionally organize spiritual retreats. People who attend are the usual suspects, a distinct and predictable handful who too often resemble me: the introverted, contemplative and introspective. If retreats only draw a small proportion of seminary students, then in the wider church they would interest an even tinier minority. Are there other ways to foster spiritual growth and development? Older generations of Mennonites in churches I've pastored were usually formed by doing things together—that is, spiritually rooted corporate and physical practices such as barn-raising, quilting, hosting, disaster relief and overseas service and development work.

We need to expand understandings of spiritual practices.

Walking can be one such spiritual practice. Various religious traditions speak of "prayer walks" or walking mindfully. In church history there is a distinct Christian practice that involves moving by foot. It's called pilgrimage.

One year at the seminary, I planned a pilgrimage that involved walking twenty miles and staying overnight in a local church to honor the memory of St. Marcellus, a third century conscientious objector and martyr whose relics are deposited beneath the altar of the basilica at the University of Notre Dame. The event was a success, both in spirit and participation, and involved a number of staff and students who don't usually attend seminary retreats.

Just as I have long known I require retreats, now I realize that I deeply need to amble. And once is not enough. Almost invariably, when I go on a long hike or a spiritual retreat, I relive the same cycle that calls me back to what God longs for me, the focal living of what Jesus called the "need of only one thing . . . the better part" (Luke 10:42).

PRAYER WALKING

I now see that I long ago began meeting God on foot. Walking, I've found, is particularly conducive to prayer. It is not just accidental or circumstantial that Scriptures often speak of this as a metaphor for faithfulness.

When I was fifteen our family spent some winter weeks in the Netherlands: sightseeing, visiting relatives and connecting with my parents' roots and reminiscences. It was a terrific and memorable time. But it could also get intense, especially as my grandmother's house had no central heating. That far north, darkness came early. The five of us were cooped up together for long evenings in a small living room, warmed by the home's one heater, our ears and eyes bombarded by a loud and bright television. So every evening, I went for a long walk through the dimming streets of that Dutch town to care for my inner introvert and to process with God all I saw and experienced in the land of my ancestors.

When I was a teen growing up in a rural area, one way to cope with adolescent anxieties and turmoils was to stroll after supper and talk to God. We lived in the country, so my feet carried me through nearby fields. My prayer then was mostly one way: I poured out long-winded speeches heavenward. I looked to the sky, offering gut-wrenched pleas to God, sorting out dilemmas and questions that seemed irresolvable. I still remember the specifics of some of those internal debates and—with the intervening time—it is striking to see how unimportant some now seem and how many of them worked out well!

Back then I did not imagine that walking and prayer had much to do with each other, anymore than I might have considered whether there are other ways to pray than just telling God a lot of things that—let's face it—God already knew! For me, this was a convenient way to get out and away. It gave coveted and longed-for solitude. I had privacy.

I did not have to deal with other people for a little while. It was purely a means to worthwhile ends.

But now I see things differently. Not only do I reject the idea of walking as purely means, I also see more and more that this exercise can itself be a rich and rewarding form of prayer.

A missed emphasis of Christian faith is the call for deeper appreciation of feet and footwork. In Paul's comparison of the body of Christ to the human body in I Corinthians 12, he tosses off a line noting that the head cannot dismiss the feet with an "I have no need of you" (v. 21). And while I know that he spoke figuratively, the miracle of what feet can do also means I now need to hear this in literal ways as well and to keep giving due attention to feet and their functions.

UNBIND THESE FEET AND LET THEM GO

I had been warned about the *meseta*. This vast plain spreads westward from Burgos and takes over a week to cross by foot. It does not have the dramatic, rugged beauty of mountainous regions or wooded wilderness. Some pilgrims lament being bored here, if not worse. They suggest that the unrelenting sameness, the scarcity of trees and the daunting hugeness of the sky plays tricks with minds and undermines morale. Descriptions I read beforehand were not encouraging.

> It is dry and scorching hot in the summer, with a low population density. Pilgrims often describe feeling very alone as they walk through this zone. For some, . . . it is disconcerting or challenging. Some experience illness, vulnerability, increased fatigue, and . . . crisis. One of the characteristics of the meseta is its horizon, which appears to never end. One English pilgrim described feeling . . . psychologically undone by the meseta.

The reputation of this area is so negative that I was not surprised when

I met a number of pilgrims who decided not even to attempt that 140 miles; they rode the bus instead. I wondered what to anticipate in this area and approached it with some dread.

In Castrojeriz, on the *meseta* plain, I arrived around noon in a small stone city that baked under the sun. The outskirts of town were filled with decayed and crumbling mud-and-stone homes. Entire neighborhoods were simply abandoned; it looked like a war zone. Closer to the center of town, I found a private *refugio*. Across the street was a medieval church that had skull-and-crossbones sculptured all over its exterior walls. *Memento mori:* Remember your death. As the temperature soared over 105 degrees that day, an imminent demise was easy to ponder and believe.

It had been some days since my crisis in Burgos, and I still wore the bandages the ER nurse had put there. My one foot was so bulky with them that my boot did not fit; I had to hike with sandals instead, even as I fretted whether my ankles would hold up. I had not been permitted a shower yet, as I was supposed to keep my feet as dry as possible. Here I finally decided it was time to look them over. Once settled near my latest bunk bed, I unwrapped them cautiously and decided that apart from the impressive discoloration of the healed blood blister, the feet looked improved. Still ugly, but progressing.

I cleaned up, had a long-awaited shower and set off to find a municipal nurse to render an official verdict on my feet. The clinic was a set of cavernous rooms with high ceilings in a ramshackle building. As others consulted with doctors or nurses, I could hear everything that transpired behind the loosely rattling doors. Understanding was another thing, as it was all spoken rapid-fire. After an hour-long wait, two nurses finally gave me the complimentary medical attention pilgrims often receive. They were frustrated with my paltry Spanish and did not get any friendlier when I tried to make a connection by mentioning that my wife was a nurse. Perhaps they thought as I am married to a nurse, I should know better than to undertake this excursion. I got the feeling that they were generally fed up with crazy sojourners. But they granted permission for me to continue my journey, as long as I regularly elevated my feet, wrapped them in gauze and kept anointing them with iodine.

I set out the next morning at 5:30, my feet newly unbound, like Lazarus not-so-fresh from the tomb. Outside of town I quickly encountered a steep ridge. That was not anticipated; I thought the *meseta* was supposed to be flat. As I mounted the rising gravel pathway, my pulse quickened and my breathing became labored, a trusty machine kicking into operation. I marveled as my feet and legs propelled me upward. Near the top, I was swarmed by annoying midges (gnatlike flies) and thus did not pause too long to drink water. And soon I had to descend the other side of the ridge. The plain stretched out ahead of me; I could see the pathway curving and winding for miles, all the way to the impossibly distant horizon.

The walk that day was long and lonely, and I loved it. It gave me time to say and sing my prayers. I saw almost no one. But in the first hour while it was still dark, just up ahead of me—when I thought I was in the middle of nowhere—a tall, husky, bearded man stood off to the side studying me. Where did he come from? He had no pack. There were no vehicles near at hand. He did not look like a pilgrim. I felt a little anxious and vulnerable as I approached. But then he observed that I was *muy pronto*, "very early." "You too," *usted tambien*, I retorted, and he laughed loudly. He seemed friendly, but I was still glad to have noticed earlier that there were more pilgrims a little way behind me.

The sun rose, casting my elongated shadow ahead of me. The silhouette of my legs appeared several times as long as my torso, resembling a drawing that I might make with my limited artistic abilities.

As the geography emerged and detached itself from the night, I looked with appreciation. I did not find the *meseta* boring or distressing, daunting or dispiriting. While not pitched and peaked like mountainous areas, still it undulated with small rolling hills and unforeseen valleys. Miles of green grain fields of wheat spread out on all sides. Clumps of bright red poppies peeked between wheat shoots and sprang up in profusion along the path.

I had dreaded the *meseta*, put off by what I heard ahead of time, but I found it reliably lovely instead. I had fretted over my feet, and here they were—after a close call—working well. It was all gift and grace. This long journey of the Camino kept reversing many of my understandings and expectations.

12

—

HERE I WALK,
I CAN DO NO OTHER

Keeping Faith with Our Feet

—

You will show me the path of life;
in your presence there is fullness of joy,
and in your right hand are pleasures for evermore.

PSALM 16:11 BCP

A WALKER'S-EYE VIEW

Shortly before leaving for the Camino, I received a nifty one-page tourist map outlining the entire route. Small but charmingly and colorfully laid out, it was perfect for showing people who were curious about where the pilgrimage would take me. I used it to orient friends and family. A number of those folks expected that I would carry this map with me on my journey and expressed surprise that I had no such intention.

One reason, of course, is that I was looking to pare down and did not need extraneous materials. Every ounce counts, after all. But how does someone know what is peripheral and what is essential?

In this instance, discernment was straightforward. Such maps simply are not useful for a pedestrian. It was certainly helpful in showing others, before and after my travels, the parameters of my long-distance walk. It could perhaps prove a good aid for people planning a car journey, giving a clear sense of cities and highways. Sometimes that's all we need to know when driving.

But pedestrians require more detail and nuance. It is not enough to see major highways, especially because those are routes we prefer to avoid. (Busy, noisy traffic feels like a threatening assault when one is on foot.) A few map inches might usefully cover five hundred miles at relatively high speeds by plane, car, train or bus, but moving on one's own two legs slows one down and means that more information, far more detailed data, is required.

To that end I carried thirty-one maps, marking various stages along the way. Everyday I hung one in a plastic pouch around my neck. At the end of a day I routinely filed the map and reviewed whatever I faced tomorrow. Each sheet outlined a proposed journey that could be accomplished in six to eight hours. I did not follow these legalistically, but did end up traveling thirty-one days.

These maps showed not just major cities and highways but also smaller paths, little villages, noteworthy landmarks, elevations, directions, turns and water fountains. I particularly appreciated that they helped me gauge distances, and I thus carefully planned my days, especially meals and lodging. As I journeyed, I was encouraged by a sense of progress made and diminishing distance to cover.

Walkers need different kinds of maps than drivers or riders. The world looks and feels different on foot than in a vehicle. Cars flatten experience of the earth: while you can't help noticing serious hills, many slopes are not perceived. With cruise control, you may hear the engine work harder, but even going uphill or down feels pretty much the same.

On foot, I might become aware that here is not just a different grade but also another microclimate. On my daily four-mile jaunt at home, for example, one block is consistently windier and colder than the rest of my route. I would not know that if I remained sheltered in a vehicle. Walking, I may not just see a patch of flowers or clover but smell it too. Or I might find a tree with juicy mulberries. Such delights are seldom experienced from inside a car.

The first day that I began hiking the Bruce Trail, the route was enormously rewarding and the scenery breathtaking. Large, old trees towered overhead. I marveled at gargantuan limestone boulders that threatened to break off and plummet down high cliffs. I was awed by lovely glades. What struck me even more than the beauty of these vistas is that they were within a mile or two of where I lived out my teenage years. They were there all along, but I had never seen them; my movements and views were confined to an automobile. I saw nature through screens: outside it was the windshield, inside a television. (Now it is often by a computer monitor.) Ironically, I could spend hours captivated at home by glittering TV images of nature but did not bother to walk a mile or two to engage the bountiful beauty in our own backyard.

More and more I've noticed that when I see an interesting area, one of my first questions now is, What would it be like to walk there? If *saunter* really does stem from *Saint Terre*, then by using my own two feet I am learning to honor and cherish the holiness of place—many places in fact.

Moving at the Speed of Life

I also know that my watch moves more slowly when I am on foot. Walking affects not just space and distance but also time itself. In our high-speed way of living—which we intriguingly call "driven"—we miss many things. Christian faith calls us to a different pace of life, and walking is a vital way to achieve that.

When I began hiking I noticed that my excursion days felt long, whether I tried to cover eight, twelve or sixteen or more miles. I moved at my own speed on those unstructured endeavors, taking breaks as needed and exploring whatever catches my attention. But it was not just the relaxed pace of walking that transformed my sense of time. On some of my best hiking days I began early in the morning and was home by mid-afternoon. The rest of the day felt ample too. On the Camino, many of us began at 5:30 a.m. to beat the sun's heat and were finished by noon or early afternoon. We had done a full day's work by then. But that was followed by a leisurely afternoon and evening for laundry and food and plenty of space for visiting, reading, napping and journaling. Each dawn-to-dusk actually felt like two long, luxurious days.

In an essay titled "Time by Design," Linda Breen Pierce argues that driving exposes us "to both faster speeds and greater stimulation" than walking. Consequently the brain must "work harder as you focus on safety and process all that you see." It pressures us with "a rush of sensory perceptions." Walking, then, is not just physically slower but mentally as well. There is less to take in, to process, to absorb. And we are able to deal with what faces us. On Sundays, when I walk to church, the half hour on foot enriches my preparedness for and experience of worship. Sundays are a premium for me. I work hard all week, but this is a day, a sabbath, to be freed from work and worry. It may seem surprising that I can spare thirty precious minutes each way. But the days that I drive and "save" time pass more quickly and consequently feel harried, hurried, hasty and hectic.

An acquaintance lost his driving permit after one legal infraction too many. It was a serious offense, and he was not allowed to drive for years. Because of this, as a middle-aged man he had to walk two miles to work. This is not something he would have chosen himself, but it beat breaking the law or the cumulative expense of a taxi.

And he made a discovery. As he went to work in the morning, he had time to prepare himself for the shift ahead. He could anticipate challenges of the day and psyche himself up to face whatever he might have to do. Rather than go to his job at the last minute, barely having woken up, rushing his breakfast and driving to work, he got there collected and composed. Things went better for him.

At the end of the day he reversed the process as he sauntered home. This was an opportunity to review what had happened. To debrief himself about intense experiences or emotions. To let go and set aside unfinished business that troubled him. And when he got home, he was fully there, completely available to his family. Walking helped him to be present to his work and to his kin, each in its own sphere. It was a good phase in his life.

Technological culture—in spite of "labor-saving" rhetoric and devices—actually makes us busier. Pauses, breaks and respites have disappeared. The norm of multitasking leaves us unaware of what goes on within or around us. But walking can move us into a different mode. Einstein showed that time is relative. Moving on our own two feet has its own pace; I call it the speed of life.

Pierce argues that time can be "dead" or "live." In the former, one does something "not inherently pleasurable, fulfilling, or satisfying." Think of commuting or fighting traffic jams. (No wonder that walking the Camino caused many to reexamine their occupations.) The soul-killing boredom of driving is evidenced by the popularity of using cell phones or personal entertainment devices while underway. Driving is an activity that is almost always merely a means to an end. Live time, however, is worthwhile in itself; it is enjoyable with its own internal, intrinsic goods. In walking, the means is as valuable and worthwhile as the goal itself. It teaches us to pay more attention to live time and to prioritize building that into our lives. Walking, as Borgmann might say, is in every sense focal.

Theologian Kosuke Koyama presses this notion of appropriate speed even further. He suggests that some things God can teach us only very slowly, at the pace of walking, the speed of life. He marvels that Israelites needed forty years of trekking through the desert. They learned "the word of God in the wilderness as they walked three miles an hour" with "the three mile an hour God."

HERE I WALK: I CAN DO NO OTHER

Yet driving is now normal and respectable; hoofing it is not. One of our international students loves to stroll. He often finds himself the only one out and about. "How nice," he says, "that Elkhart built sidewalks just for me." Frequently as he wanders, strangers taunt and mock him. Pedestrians are suspect, of questionable status: those who cannot afford cars or are not able to drive, perhaps the unemployed or the mentally handicapped.

When driving is so convenient, no wonder many choose that option. Peter Maurin and Dorothy Day, founders of the Catholic Worker movement, used to speak of creating a society where it is easier to be and do good. In our culture it is less trouble to drive than to walk, even if that choice is wasteful and unhealthy. Strolling is actually discouraged. The street where I live has neither shoulders nor sidewalks, so being on foot is unpleasant and even dangerous. More than once I jumped onto a lawn to miss getting hit by speeding drivers who pass others illegally on the right.

I could name dozens of people who drive an hour or two each day to and from work and think nothing of it. It is the price they pay for a job. But I know hardly anyone who walks thirty minutes for their commute, let alone an hour or two. How strange we would regard someone who did that, even though it is far healthier physically, emotionally, spiritually and environmentally. An acquaintance walks for pleasure up to two hours a day and is sheepish about it. It is not usual behavior, after all. But who apologizes about spending that much time watching television, playing computer games or surfing the World Wide Waste of time?

Walking is an act of dissent; it is countercultural.

One winter morning back home, my wife and I left church after the service—and had to proceed on the street because of all the snow on unshoveled sidewalks. We stepped boldly onto the road and I realized: "This is a protest."

Indeed, walking is a demonstration, a demurral against flagrant expenditure of nonrenewable resources. In opposition to the noise of motor vehicles. Counter to the ugliness of cities and communities shaped to accommodate cars and discourage pedestrians. In opposition to all the burying of topsoil under asphalt. Mourning for how long one has to go before feet can touch the earth. In remonstration against the danger that cars pose. And on and on.

As I made my little declaration of dissent, I realized that I was not angry. I was joyful and sad, both at once. Gladdened by the opportunity to walk and regretting that others did not know what they were missing.

Whatever you consider perfect weather for walking, this day probably was not it. The wind-chill factor was around zero degrees Fahrenheit, meaning standing still is going to hurt. The temperature was on the opposite end of the thermometer from my pilgrimage in Spain. But while the weather was different, both the Camino and being on foot to and from church are in the spirit of pilgrimage.

Nevertheless, to make matters worse, even though a Canadian should know better, I had neglected to wear long johns. My thin Sunday-go-to-church pants did not provide much barrier or insulation against the chill. Sidewalks were full of snow, and so we had to proceed on the roads. They were slipperier than usual, given the wintry conditions. Thus we worried not just about staying on our own two feet but also about whether drivers could control cars on the icy surfaces.

Protesting is well and good, and I've engaged in it some, but I'm not sure that would have been enough motivation to get me out that day. Anger, even rage, can carry us only so far. Besides, if walking is just a protest, then it is reduced to a mere means to an end. Too much of our technological culture, as Albert Borgmann eloquently argues, reduces everything, not just objects but people and relationships and practices as well, to devices. Devices are expected to produce solitary and obvious products, results or commodities. How shallow that makes life.

We had just left a powerfully rich worship service. The music stirred the congregation. The gospel challenged and inspired us to faithfulness. We saw good friends, sisters and brothers in Christ. I escorted a small, trusting neighbor child to the front and got to hug and hold him for the children's story. We prayed for troubled and hurting places around the world. We had a direct engagement with children, teachers and the principal from the inner-city school down the block from our church, with whom our congregation is in long-term partnership.

What was the single-most important product or commodity from that worship? The question is nonsensical. The interweaving web of goods exponentially enriched everyone in ways that could never be graphed or tabulated, calculated or counted.

Likewise the walk to and from church. It was fine to be out in that fierce winter and to generate enough body heat by moving steadily to keep ourselves at least comfortable if not warm. (I once heard someone note that only drivers complain about the cold; it certainly amazes me how long people run their cars to warm them before setting out.)

Lorna and I had leisurely time to visit along the way, and we both thought of important things to tell each other, matters that had somehow eluded us in the busyness of the previous week. We reveled in an all-too-rare day of winter sunshine in northern Indiana. I felt good, whole, alive and radiant.

As we walked, the sun shone on wind-sculpted snowdrifts, which sparkled as if they were full of precious diamonds. That only happens when it is severely cold. And the best way to see it is on foot. Who says protesting has to be a downer? If Catherine of Siena was right that "all the way to heaven is heaven," then surely anything that is now part of our faithful pilgrimage will already be richly rewarding and evoke glimpses of heaven for us.

Above and Below

While walking, I often tune into inspiration and meaning I'd not otherwise notice. In my prayers on the Camino I thought about the relationship between God's dwelling place of heaven and ours here on earth. Praying the Lord's Prayer many times each day, I was repeatedly struck by the phrase "on earth as in heaven." I looked at vast and beautiful surroundings and yearned for God's good earth to know God's hope and redemption. On the path those spheres seemed closer than ever. I moved on the cusp of them both.

While walking I chanted the classic doxology. My feet rhythmically tapped the earth, a metronome pacing my song:

Praise God from whom all blessings flow;
Praise God all creatures here below;
Praise God above ye heavenly hosts;
Praise Father, Son and Holy Ghost.
Amen.

Heaven—"above ye heavenly hosts"—and earth—"here below"—are linked, especially as we step on God's earth and prayers ascend from here to God's throne. We sometimes deride people for being "so heavenly minded that they are no earthly good." Here I found that walking on earth linked me to heaven.

Never in my life have I felt so strongly that connection. Celtic Christians once spoke of "thin places," where the veil separating the present and eternity was flimsier than usual. Is the Camino a thin place? Or has it just become so, worn to translucence by the persistent presence of many pilgrims? Which came first, the thin place or the pilgrim?

Being firmly grounded, touching the earth with every step, feeling the demands of traveling this most basic way, I felt as close to heaven as I can ever remember. Being outside was key to this sensibility. This is not so surprising for a Christian. As Wendell Berry writes:

> I don't think it is enough appreciated how much an outdoor book the Bible is. It is a . . . book open to the sky. It is best read and understood outdoors, and the farther outdoors the better. . . . Passages that within walls seem improbable or incredible, outdoors seem merely natural. . . .
>
> What the Bible might mean, or how it could mean anything, in a closed, air-conditioned building, I do not know.

Indeed, Scriptures rely heavily on the outdoors. The psalms reflect extensively on images of the beauty and majesty of God's creation and order. How many parables would be left if we excised all references to the natural world, sun or seed, wheat or weed? Think of the importance of gardens and deserts and seas and rivers in Scripture. Or of how often Jesus deliberately went to mountain tops or wilderness or the water.

I go further than Berry. It is not only that we cannot read and understand Scripture inside; I suspect that even our praise of God is hampered there. Eugene Peterson cautions us about our comfortable, overly technologized way of life as a sphere where "the wonder has leaked out." I discovered on the Camino that being *alfresco* inspires prayer and praise.

However, it was not just being outside. In Acts 3 a lame man is healed and began "walking and leaping and praising God" (v. 8). My long journey convinces me that it is no coincidence that these verbs are parallel. Worship of God is closely bound up with the wonder of walking.

CONCLUSION

—

This God is our God for ever and ever;
he shall be our guide for evermore.

PSALM 48:13 BCP

WHERE THE SAINTS GO MARCHING IN

My last night before reaching Santiago was one of the most unpleasant. The dormitory was several stories tall and housed hundreds in its crowded rooms. Although sponsored by the government rather than by volunteers and charitable agencies, it was ill-kept and filthy, the worst one of the entire trip. I made the mistake of looking under my bed when I left the next morning to see whether I had left anything behind and was repulsed by the accumulated grime and trash there. "No more of this," I consoled myself. "When I get to Santiago, I will rent a proper room."

It was Sunday morning, and many pilgrims were anxious to get to the Santiago cathedral for the morning mass. Like them, I left early. But I knew that the tendonitis hobbling my right leg would not allow me the necessary speed to get there on time for the worship service. I resolved not even to try.

The trip was slow-going. Every swing forward of my right leg hurt.

Eager pilgrims passed me all morning. I was glad to be nearing the end of my formidable journey but still wondered whether I could do it. This was the most painful walking yet, and there were moments when I thought I might faint. It brought to mind that plaintive if corny jazz standard "Feet Don't Fail Me Now."

After a couple hours of trudging I stopped for a drink and a snack. I was surprised to see my friend Markus, the physiotherapist, walking jauntily along toward me. We'd both splurged and eaten hamburgers for supper the night before; for the first time on that journey I had a craving for North American food. Our burgers tasted so good that we ordered seconds. Perhaps my psyche was already preparing to return home.

Pleased to see Markus approach, I didn't even secretly judge him for chatting on a cell phone while moving. He was eagerly reporting to Susanne, his significant other at home in Germany, how close he was to Santiago, the goal of his walking. He stopped, and we chatted awhile. He took my camera and snapped one of my favorite photos of me from the trip: I am wearing my backpack, arms and face tanned, eyes squinting from the effort of the trip, beard as long as it's ever been in my life, hands clutching my walking stick and my shirt damp with perspiration. But I am smiling.

Markus was willing to keep a slow pace with me. But I knew that he was keen to get to the mid-morning service. I urged him to go on without me. (We met up in the city later that day and had a fine *pulpo* supper together.)

As I walked, I realized that distance had played a trick on me again. I had assumed that Santiago was still far off, but fourteen miles is not long by car and city terms. And so a good part of the way was like walking through suburb after suburb, not the most inspirational of views. Give me the *meseta* any day.

In the last hour, for some reason, my leg stopped hurting. Finally I came to a crest of a hill and could see Santiago down below, the medieval structures of the old city glimpsed between the low skyline of modern buildings. And so I walked and kept walking. Eventually I came to the old city and followed its maze of winding cobblestone streets.

I arrived at the main Cathedral plaza late in the morning. The vast courtyard was crowded with pilgrims and sightseers, locals and entrepreneurial buskers. It had the festive aura of a carnival. As I finally glimpsed the front façade of the cathedral, whose photo I'd seen many times before now, I felt some measure of disbelief. What was even more striking, however, was that people—strangers all—cheered and clapped for me and each person following me. The steady stream of straggling pilgrims arriving in that famous space was greeted with applause.

Sunday morning services were finished, and I found myself reluctant to go into the cathedral, even though I had been planning to come to this place for years. The lines looked long—Sundays are its busiest days—and I did not feel ready yet for some reason.

I went to the crowded cathedral office to receive my Compostela certificate. I found a pay phone and called Lorna out of bed. (Later, during sharing time at our church, she would announce my safe arrival.)

A block from the cathedral, I discovered reasonably priced accommodations with a private washroom and shower. The tiny room was packed with an end table, wooden cupboard and narrow bed. A foot-and-a-half wide aisle ran between the bed and the cupboard, leading to the bathroom. There was not enough space on the floor for my backpack. I emptied the cupboard of its pillow and blankets and stashed my knapsack there, although the door would not completely shut. Still it was clean and private, and all seemed unimaginably luxurious after a month on the road.

For the rest of the day I visited with acquaintances I ran into, and a few times peeked into the cathedral but was still put off by the crowds there. The next morning, however, I was ready and went to the Pilgrims' Mass. Here I was at last, worshiping where so many believers had been before me. I remembered words from T. S. Eliot's "Little Gidding." (Little Gidding is a place of pilgrimage in Britain.)

You are here to kneel
Where prayer has been valid.

Later, after the service, I would look carefully at all the items associated with the apostle James. Some of them perplexed me, especially the *Matamoros* imagery. Still, I was awestruck by the immense cruciform cathedral, and in the following days I went there often to wander and to pray. I could never find a way to capture this Romanesque edifice's vast expanse and its fifty towering columns with my camera.

The priest welcomed pilgrims. At the start of each service, a list of the new arrivals is read. Shivers ran through me when he announced one Canadian having arrived by foot from St. Jean. And that was me. It was true; I was here.

As the service proceeded there were two populations present. Chairs were crowded with those of us wanting to worship. Many backpacks were lined up along the walls. But others kept roaming aisles and studying statues. Some of those distracted folks were pilgrims with packs, still wandering and walking. Yet the chaos did not feel out of place.

A nun in a modest dark blue habit confidently led the congregational singing. Many songs were familiar ones from Taizé, so I was able to join. Her voice was hauntingly beautiful. This was a highlight for me. One of my colleagues, Marlene Kropf, argues that singing is a sacrament for Mennonites. Even my non-Christian friends commented on the worshipful quality of the music here. The priest's sermon was lengthy and mostly incomprehensible for me. (Actually, I never understood any of the Spanish homilies I heard that month; the words went by too fast and used theological vocabulary that I had not acquired.)

As communion was offered in the crowded aisles, servers stood under festive and colorful umbrellas so that they could be spotted and found from afar. I felt a twinge of sadness, knowing that I as a Protestant was not welcome to participate in this Roman Catholic celebration. But I did not feel completely alone.

THE GREAT CLOUD OF WITNESSES

After the Pilgrims' Mass was finished, I busily greeted people in the congregation whom I had come to know in the last weeks. I was not always sure of their faith stance, but I was glad to see them in this church. During the service, many of us had been catching each other's eyes and acknowledging one another. There was an air of euphoria. The journey was done. Now we could relax and celebrate. Several times as I moved through the crowd I was caught off-guard by people I encountered long ago and had figured I would never meet again. I was especially happy to see Jean-Louis; he'd traveled one thousand miles in all. I did not call him *vous*. But we were even; he did not greet me with a Frenchman's raspberry either.

Only a few days into the trip I noticed the delight of familiar faces. How good it felt to come into a *refugio* and see someone I'd run into before, shared a meal with or even a bench while resting. Or to relax in a hostel and have a recognizable face appear. It did not matter whether we'd ever conversed or even knew each other's names. There was a deep reassurance just in sighting a pilgrim I'd glimpsed earlier.

I came to count on this kind of boost and missed it when it did not happen. A week before arriving in Santiago, I was separated from a group I had walked with for a few days. That evening I entered a *refugio* and saw not one soul that I'd ever met or observed, even though I'd been traveling for weeks. That contributed to the feeling of having a bad day.

Santiago, however, was a small foretaste of heaven. There was tremendous excitement at reconnecting with people from all along the Camino, even folks I had not seen since the first few days. I imagine the afterlife to be an opportunity to catch up with those I've lost touch with along the way: friends and family, brothers and sisters in the faith, casual acquaintances, and even historical saints who inspired me from afar.

Strolling around the city, I watched for familiar faces. I studied everyone I passed or who passed me. I paid special attention to obvious pilgrims—and there were many—carrying backpacks. Sometimes, I would think, *I know that person*, but was unable to place him or her exactly.

I was not the only one. From Santiago I made a one-day bus excursion with other sojourners to see the mysterious Atlantic coastline at Finisterre, "the end of the earth." Some pilgrims chose to walk that farther sixty miles. Whenever our vehicle passed a trekker, it was as if the whole bus leaned over, since all of us riding pilgrims turned to see whether we recognized that particular person on foot.

Even more fun was sitting at an outdoor table in Santiago, eyeing people who passed. Almost invariably, recognized folk appeared. It was difficult to sustain a conversation with one person on the street or at table as acquaintances kept showing up and the visiting expanded to include them too.

It was essential to speak to other pilgrims. We shared our joy and offered congratulations on this accomplishment. Or commiserated with those few who were not able to complete it physically and had resigned themselves to arriving by bus.

With some folks a brief street conversation was enough. With others it was important to have a final meal together. Table fellowship and hospitality are so vital to Christian faith—and apparently will be important in eternity too—so this as well seemed eschatological.

But Santiago is not heaven, of course. In fact, there were rumors of theft and warnings to watch our possessions and backpacks. We could not leave things lying around, propped in the street against store or restaurant walls, as we had for the last five hundred miles.

And there were other bittersweet moments too. Jane plunged immediately into a deep depression because she had met her years-long goal and she did not know what to aim for next. Jeff had a kidney stone episode days before arriving in Santiago; he had to take vehicles to complete his journey and thus did not merit the official cathedral Compostela certifying completion of the pilgrimage. He had been praying for his father and somehow this anticlimactic conclusion seemed to diminish his devotion. Both pilgrims had meaningful visits with other sojourners nevertheless.

There was other sadness too. Many meals were "last suppers." In most cases we knew that we would never see this person again, at least not in this life. We were from all around the world and would soon disperse in far-flung directions. It is not possible to maintain contact with everyone. So while the reminiscing was good, it was also haunted by the awareness that we would soon part and say goodbye to folks who shared one of my life's most rewarding achievements.

I Could Walk Five Hundred Miles

Some years ago the Proclaimers, a Scottish group, sang a catchy tune outlandishly promising to the latest love of their life that they would gladly walk five hundred miles for her. It's a familiar love song motif: boasting of daunting acts of courage and bravado to prove devotion and commitment. I always liked to sing along to that jaunty song, even though its sentiment seemed unlikely. But now, having walked five hundred miles myself, it no longer appears so outlandish.

Over and again my journals reflect both hardship and gratitude on this journey. More than once I note—often with surprise—that I feel "deeply happy." The joy was sparked by simple things: good conversations and welcome companionship, ample if simple food, a shower (preferably warm) and a bed during the night (near a window guaranteed some fresh air while sleeping). The joy also reflected my appreciation for the physical ability just to be able to accomplish such a journey. This spirit of contentment was not only about each day's travels, however.

Fifty times a day I quietly and meditatively sang a Taizé verse:

Bless the Lord,
my soul
And bless God's holy name
Bless the Lord, my soul,
who leads me into life.

I learned this favorite piece from a visit to the community of Taizé years earlier. Now I was particularly taken by the last phrase: God "leads me into life." This rang true and was deeply meaningful on several counts.

I daily reviewed my life on this trip and felt deep gratitude for opportunities and experiences, family and friends. I saw that my years had been touched by God in ways too many to count.

This was no naive enumeration. I revisited disappointments, disillusionments, sorrows, griefs and betrayals as well. I took a hard look at major failures and mistakes over the years. I noticed that matters that had once preoccupied and obsessed me now were in a different place within. I was calm; I was at peace. Not that I appreciated everything that had happened to me or had been done to me, and certainly I was not smug about where I had gone wrong.

Rather, I had perspective. I could recognize how God was at work, even in those hardest of times. I often did not see God's hand at the moment—or even long afterward—but I could now. I had a sense of God's providence, even in the greatest tragedies and hardest eras. I could relate to Joseph's powerfully profound words to his brothers when he assured them of his forgiveness because of trust in God's providence. In spite of the terrible traumas he suffered, he was able to say to them: "Do not be afraid! Am I in the place of God? Even though you intended to do harm to me, God intended it for good. . . . So have no fear" (Genesis 50:19-21).

Because of the Camino, I grew in my ability to see God's larger purposes at work. I can embrace a quote from Meister Eckhart that I heard at a low point years ago: "Whatever happens to you is the best possible thing for your salvation." Yes, God led and leads me into life.

ARRIVING WHERE WE BEGAN

Pilgrimage reflects the faith journey, even as it deepens and reinforces one's walk with God. I could perceive the divine hand in my opportunity to be on the Camino, in hard lessons learned along the way, in the chance to know more about myself and to encounter many different pilgrims. Here too God led me into life. Thus I returned home filled with gratitude.

Yet questions remained. How would I be when I went back? Had I changed? Had I learned anything? Would insights gleaned inform and affect me? In my final few days, as I savored Santiago, I had a challenging dream. I remember none of the content, only a refrain I heard over and over: "I walk at the intersection of the true Camino and real life." Ultimately, pilgrimage bears fruit at home where it overlaps and infiltrates and alters one's life. Christian pilgrimage reorients normal, day-to-day existence.

Still, Celtic saint Abbess Samantham warned against making an idol of such practices: "Since God is near to all who call upon him, we are under no obligation to cross the sea. The kingdom of heaven can be reached from every land." If we think God or the holy are only else-where, then pilgrimage misleads us. Rather, we are called to see all our surroundings—even normal, routine places—with new eyes.

On the transatlantic flight home I was eager for the chance to watch my first film in weeks. There, a phrase from T. S. Eliot was improbably but providentially quoted by a character played by John Travolta:

> We shall not cease from exploration
> And the end of all our exploring
> Will be to arrive where we started
> And know the place for the first time.

"We shall not cease exploration"; we are always sojourners moving along the way, not just when we are official pilgrims. That ongoing restless wandering perpetually brings us back home to ourselves. Just as the Camino showed me more deeply things I already knew about myself, so it invited me to be acquainted with my home and life in new ways, "for the first time." As Scott Russell Sanders notes: "Pilgrims often journey to the ends of the earth in search of holy ground, only to find that they have never walked on anything else."

I remain deeply thankful for the privilege of this providential pil-grimage. I pray the Camino bears fruit so that indeed "I will *walk* in the presence of the LORD" (Psalm 116:8 BCP, emphasis added).

Appendix I

RECOVERING AND RECLAIMING CHRISTIAN PILGRIMAGE

A pilgrimage is a journey undertaken in the light of a story.
A great event has happened; the pilgrim hears the reports and goes in search of
evidence, aspiring to be an eyewitness. The pilgrim seeks not only to confirm the
experience of others firsthand but to be changed by the experience.

Pilgrimages are connected to events, stories and narratives of places or people where God has been active or encountered. Celtic Christian traditions of "thin places" hold that in some locations God feels somehow more readily accessible. Christian pilgrimage, then, has to do with going to particular locations to situate oneself within God's story among us, so that we too might be touched—even transformed or converted—by salvation history, God's metanarrative. Seeing and directly engaging such sites is a way of appropriating the story for oneself.

There were always critics of pilgrimage, including Gregory of Nyssa (fourth century), Wycliffe (fourteenth century) and Erasmus (fifteenth century), to name just a few. There were abuses of pilgrimage, to be sure. The Reformation certainly tapped into longstanding suspicions and legitimate critiques. But there were rich and significant theological understandings at work in pilgrimage practices all along as well.

SURVEYING CHRISTIAN PILGRIMAGE

By the early centuries of the church certain believers concerned about the comfortable and established ways of Christians in the Roman Empire headed to the wilderness—from Egypt to Syria and places in between. Desert fathers' and mothers' lives were full of uncertainty and challenge, and bore witness to God's purposes and God's reign. They took godly sojourning and resident-alien status literally.

Around the same time, Christians from afar—including desert fathers and mothers—began visiting holy Christians, exemplary monks, in Palestine. Pilgrims later went there to be in touch with sites associated with Jesus and biblical events. Two of the most famous fourth-century pilgrims were Helena, mother of Constantine, and Egeria, a Spanish nun. While such journeying seems obvious to us now, it was a startling innovation at the time. Some had long avoided Palestine, believing Jerusalem was "cursed, since it was the site of the Crucifixion."

A few centuries later many Celts, inspired by desert traditions, cut loose their ties of security and wandered the earth to proclaim the gospel and to live more fully by trusting God's providence. Columbanus affirmed perpetual unsettledness: "Therefore let this principle abide with us, that on the road we so live as travelers, as pilgrims, as guests of the world," and "Let us concern ourselves with things divine, and as pilgrims ever sigh for and desire our homeland . . . for the end of our roadway is our home." In the Irish legend of Brendan the Navigator, a Christian explorer puts himself in God's hands and randomly sails the seas.

Another Celtic saint, Columba, was banished from his beloved Ireland for reasons that are not clear. (As a bibliophile, I am fond of the version that has him thrown out because of a fight over a book!) Exile was the punishment for his unspecified sin. Penitential pilgrimages were often connected to the story of Cain's banishment as a "fugitive and a wanderer on the earth" (Genesis 4:12). Columba ended up on the isle of Iona, the first place where he could no longer see his cherished homeland. There he established a noteworthy monastic community, whose missionary influence extended across Scotland, well into England and continental Europe. His penitential sojourn became evangelistic. (And Iona is now once again a pilgrimage destination. See appendix three.)

Yet Celts were also duly wary of and cautious about pilgrimages. An eighth-century Irish church leader—in a culture that loved wandering—cautioned against trying to find God in travel if you did not know God more intimately, wherever you happened to be: "To go to Rome means great toil and little profit. The [heavenly] king whom you seek can only be found there if you bring him within yourself."

We saw in chapter one how the tradition of pilgrimage shrines began, but of course not everyone could go on extensive and expensive journeys to Santiago, Palestine or Rome. Labyrinths (now experiencing a revival) and Stations of the Cross emerged as local, accessible, affordable and alternative forms of portable devotion for people who were unable to travel to far-off lands.

Some religious orders, Franciscans and Dominicans, took up itinerant ministry and wandered as a primary means of missions and evangelism. Francis of Assisi said in his *Later Rule:* "As pilgrims and strangers in this world who serve the Lord in poverty and humility, let them go begging for alms with full trust." In the sixteenth century, Jesuits also impressively modeled "a spirituality of mission and mobility." (Movable and itinerant ministry was later embraced by Methodists too.)

Tom Wright's *The Way of the Lord: Christian Pilgrimage Today* shows how and why Protestants, especially evangelicals, lost sight of the merits of pilgrimage. He argues biblically and theologically for reclaiming this vital practice. His conviction about this came about only gradually; at first his Protestant inclinations made him suspicious of pilgrimage traditions. He cites potential problems and dangers with such practices: they are not necessary, they are easily subject to commercial exploitation, and Christianity is not territorial. Nevertheless, he notes three primary benefits of pilgrimages: they are excellent ways to teach and learn, they stimulate and invite prayer, they offer opportunity for growing in Christian faith and faithfulness.

> We go on the pilgrim way, we follow the way of the Lord, because he himself is the way—and, as he said himself, the truth and the life as well. We go to meet him afresh, to share his agony, and to pray and work for the victory he won on the cross to be implemented, and for his way to be followed, in . . . our own countries, and in the whole world.

Citing the work of Alan Morinis, Camino anthropologist Nancy Frey notes several types of Christian pilgrimages: *devotional*, "encounter with, and honoring of, the shrine divinity, personage, or symbol"; *initiatory*, expecting to be renewed or changed; *instrumental*, looking for results, perhaps a healing; *normative*, following a faith's "ritual calendar"; *wandering*, having "no predetermined goal." She sees all these themes in Camino practices and makes a compelling case that each of them is derived from Scripture.

TOURISM OR PILGRIMAGE?

Scholars argue over whether there are differences between tourism and pilgrimage. Various Camino authors struggle with this as well. One pilgrim, Lee Hoinacki, worried: "The prostitution of foreign and exotic places and people in order to entertain the affluent is surely a despicable use of the other. I fall asleep, troubled. Am I, too, a tourist?"

It is most helpful to see tourism and pilgrimage on a spectrum. Obviously they have much in common. They involve movement or travel. They are a break from everyday life and realities. They often involve some kind of expense. They are a privilege.

Yet several factors make these modes of movement distinct as well:

- Pilgrimage is religious, devotional or spiritual. Tourism can be secular. Still, just as more and more people are interested in ecotourism, there is now something called "spiritual tourism."

- Pilgrimage has a purpose, goal and destination of meeting and encountering God and God's truths. In some cases Christian pilgrimage (for example, among Celtic saints) meant throwing oneself on God's providential happenstance, but even then there is a purpose, that is, relying on God and God's direction. Tourism can be aimless.

- Pilgrimage involves, challenges and even changes the pilgrim. Tourism can be more objective, detached and observational.

- Pilgrimage may be lengthy and in-depth; extended experience might lead to new insights and even transformation. Tourism, however, may involve nothing more than sightseeing.

- Pilgrimage is a discipline involving spiritual practices, such as prayer, for greater focus. Tourism can be casual and recreational.

Thus pilgrimage is at its best "goal-centered, religious travel for an efficacious purpose." And Christian pilgrimage explicitly focuses on encountering and following Jesus, growing in discipleship.

Critics of pilgrimage rightly observe that we need not travel far to seek or find God. Indeed all of life can be—and ought to be—pilgrimage. Every time we venture to church, we make a small pilgrimage. Each day's activities and all our encounters can also lead us in the search for God and the longing to keep company with God. So, weekly worship and daily life ought also be done in a pilgrim spirit. Nevertheless, there is merit in deliberately engaging in more demanding journeys from time to time, just as there are good reasons to set aside certain periods for prayer, days for worship, fasting and retreat.

ELEMENTS OF PILGRIMAGE

Elements of pilgrimage then could include:

- Travel and dislocation to an unfamiliar place.

- Suspension of regular responsibilities and routines.

- Freeing and disconnecting from familiar demands of work, television, Internet, media, cell phones or other technology. An important aspect of pilgrimage is moving into liminality. This means to live beyond normal boundaries and structures of life: status, income, age or class. It also involves proceeding at a different pace. "The pilgrim slows down, moves in God's time. A pilgrimage is a conversion from 'road rage and rush' to walking unhurried and thoughtfully."

- Implementing disciplines that help us focus on God and God's priorities.

- Often sacrifices are involved. A pilgrimage may cost time, money or effort. If we do not enter a pilgrimage lightly or casually, we may be more likely to mean it and benefit from it.

- Pilgrimages may be psychologically and spiritually taxing as well. For example, "The Camino is a process which can enable a person's psychic barriers to weaken so that reality can filter through." Pilgrimages may test and stretch us; we humans often learn and grow better by engaging demanding disciplines.

- Destinations are often inconveniently located, difficult to reach. Residents on the Scottish isle of Iona boast with a smile that it is easier to get from London to Spain than from London to Iona. Geographically peripheral pilgrimage locations remind us that pilgrims may be socially marginal or countercultural.

- The pilgrim goes with a spirit of openness, hoping to encounter God and anticipating the growth that this encounter invites. Pilgrimages are not done casually but require time to prepare and ready oneself.

Appendix 2

Planning A Christian Pilgrimage

Perhaps you are drawn to a figure from church history, or a place or region fascinates you. Maybe you read about an intriguing possibility. A friend or church group could invite you to join a journey.

Pilgrimage can grow from all kinds of motives: need for rest, realization that something about your faith has grown dull or stale, facing a transition, trying to process a major crisis, longing for healing or resolution, inexplicable attraction to a particular sojourn, desire for more intense prayer, yearning to explore and better understand your beliefs, wanting to review your life or set a new course.

Preparing for Pilgrimage

As you begin to sense a possible pilgrimage call, test and discern it. Take it up in prayer. Talk it over in your small group, with your closest family, with your spiritual director. Journal about it.

As part of discernment begin researching the possible pilgrimage. Read articles or books written on the subject. Speak to others who have been to that particular place. Search the Web for information. Many destinations have links to listserves (electronic mailing lists) of previous pilgrims. Such discernment also helps with preparation.

One thing you will want to decide is whether to do and initiate this by yourself or join an organized group.

As you move more into preparation mode, tell trusted believers what you plan and why. Name reasons for going and niggling uncertainties or fears that you bring. Ask them to pray for you while you are away. When I went on the Camino pilgrimage, Nina Lanctot, a friend and pastor, collected shells and passed them among members of my small group, asking my friends to use those items as reminders to keep me in their prayers while I was away.

Have your church or small group bless you before you go. This might be part of sharing time during church worship. Or perhaps a circle of people important to you could gather before you leave: sing hymns, pray, name the call in the pilgrimage and its potential challenges. Invite the intercessions of others: ask God for strength and for protection from temptations. Close with a blessing for your journey. If possible, bring pilgrimage symbols or clothing along to this ceremonial send-off.

One of the most significant aspects of the overall program of Goshen College in Indiana is its Study-Service Term. Most students participate in this intense semester abroad, learning language skills, studying a foreign culture and contributing service to their host location. These life-changing experiences resemble pilgrimages. One reason they are effective is that the entire college is involved in sending off the travelers and welcoming them back as well. No matter what time folks leave or return—even in the wee hours of the morning—a good part of the wider campus community shows up for hugs, laughter and tears, singing and praying, farewells and blessings. Don't underestimate the power of corporate support for pilgrimage.

Decide ahead of time which spiritual disciplines you will embrace. Will you use a prayerbook? Sing certain songs? (Find all the pieces in your hymnal that use "pilgrim" metaphors; you might be surprised how many there are.) Journal? Reflect on certain themes during your prayers? Stretch yourself by trying new or unfamiliar practices? Might you review your life? Are there certain people you want to pray for? Will you carry a special object—stone, cross, photo—to remind you to pray? Are there Bible passages or sections you will ponder? Which books—if any—will you take for reading? How will you enter into the spirit and ethos of your pilgrimage destination?

Consider whether to carry or wear a symbol that reminds you of being on a pilgrimage: a cross or a shell, prayer beads or a bracelet, a scarf or hat, badge or necklace. It will reinforce the purpose of your journey and may communicate something of your identity to others around you as well.

Ponder whether you want to leave something behind on your pilgrimage. One Camino tradition has people bring stones from their homeland and leave them at the Cruz de Ferro (a longstanding iron cross encountered after climbing over a mountain range about a week away from Santiago). This symbolizes a commitment to let go of aspects of your life that hinder you from living out what God has taught you on the journey.

COMPLETING YOUR PILGRIMAGE

No pilgrimage is finished until you assimilate what happened along the way.

While pilgrimages are ostensibly about reaching a certain destination, pilgrims also often reflect more about the process itself. The way is made by walking, after all. And some find the end of their journey disappointing. Curiously, many Camino books say little—sometimes nothing—about the apostle James or the city and cathedral of Santiago de Compostela itself.

Finally arriving at your destination might prompt a number of issues. People may grieve that this exhilarating experience is now over.

Some feel particularly purposeless if they dedicated extensive time and energy to this project. *What now or next?* they may wonder. Others may not have found the journey to be quite what they expect. Or there might be sadness at having to say goodbye to companions and the intense, shared experience.

Nancy Frey discovered that many Santiago pilgrims had trouble readjusting to regular life. They encounter reentry culture shock, a "period of adjustment common to people (such as anthropologists after fieldwork, exchange students, Peace Corps workers, children after summer camp) who return home after extended stays in other countries or communities." Such dislocated awkwardness can have a number of causes.

> Daily life may not seem as relevant, exciting and open as being on the road. Moreover, the abrupt experience of return rarely allows most people to process the weeks and miles. Feeling "disoriented" is common. . . . Many miss the clear sense of direction that the Camino provides.

While the Camino pilgrimage was one of the most significant events of my life, I was surprised how hard it was to get others interested in my experience. When I mentioned it, many friends listened politely or soon changed the subject. I got the impression that this was "just another vacation" in their view. Perhaps it compares to the difficulty of explaining the highs of a retreat or conference to people "back home" who were not there.

This may be a reason why many Camino-related websites also have listserves for previous pilgrims to connect with one another.

One of the most challenging aspects of a pilgrimage is incorporating its learnings into our daily life and routines. Many pilgrim travelogues speak of lifestyle changes that authors feel called to because of such journeys. Yet it can be hard to live out those implications when faced once again at home with complex realities of friendships and family, work and school, deadlines and headlines, responsibilities and obligations, necessities of earning a living and doing housework.

In order to process and work with issues of completing and returning from a pilgrimage, consider the following questions:

- What message or themes did God give you on this journey?
- What do you want to remember well from this pilgrimage?
- What was the best aspect of this time? What was the hardest?
- How did this experience change or affect your understanding of God? Your relationship with God?
- How would you like this experience to affect your life? Or your relationship with God?
- What do you need to have the pilgrimage continue to bear fruit?

You can do a number of things with such questions and issues:

- Journal about them.
- Find other ways to remember your journey: create a photo album or scrapbook, report on the Camino to your small group or Sunday school class, write an article for the local paper or a denominational magazine.
- Pray about what you learned.
- Talk about these matters with significant others (family, spiritual friends, spiritual mentors or directors, small group).
- Testify to fellow believers about what God has done with you on this pilgrimage.
- Find ways to be accountable for what you heard from God on this venture.
- Put keepsakes or mementoes, stones or shells, art or icons, in places

of prominence in your home or workplace to help you remember.

• One Camino anthropologist believes that we do not do well at integrating pilgrimage learning into daily life as most "have no ritual of reintegration into the society we live in." Invite your friends or small group to join you in a time of worship. Share what God did through your pilgrimage and ask for prayers and support in living out the challenges ahead.

Appendix 3

Pilgrimage Destinations

Peter Walker reminds us that pilgrimage offers "the opportunity to reflect on the historical roots of one's faith and to make an appropriate, personal response." This is a way to renew and revitalize our faith. Pilgrimage is "historical enquiry bathed in prayer."

There are many places where you might choose to make a pilgrimage. Below are a number of potential destinations. This list is only suggestive. It is impossible to be comprehensive in such short space. These ideas may spark other possibilities for you. The following sections were written by friends. They name particular sites, suggest reasons why each is noteworthy and what you might want to see there. Several resources are cited as well.

Christians need to consider making pilgrimages to locations of special importance in their own particular traditions. The first entry is significant to my theological heritage, Anabaptism, which includes Mennonites. Here occurred one of our iconic Reformation stories. It speaks volumes to other Christians today as well.

Asperen, South Holland, Netherlands
by James Junhke
The village of Asperen in South Holland (Netherlands) was the home of Dirk Willems, an Anabapist martyr (d. 1569). He escaped from incarceration but stopped to rescue his drowning pursuer and

thus was captured and executed. The church tower prison, where Willems spent his last days, is still standing. A short way from the village is the Appeldijk, site of Willems's execution. There is an "Oud Asperen" town museum and a street, "Dirk Willemszstraat," named after the martyr.

Asperen is unique for the way non-Mennonites there have honored an Anabaptist martyr. It is one of the most inspirational sites for spiritual pilgrimage in Europe, yet has been largely ignored by Mennonite tour groups. Willems's story is the most famous one in the *Martyrs Mirror*, partly because the dramatic etching of the event by the Dutch artist, Jan Luykens, has been so widely reproduced.

Resources

Juhnke, James. *Dirk's Exodus.* Topeka, Kans.: Woodley Memorial Press, 1992.

————. "Dutch Villagers Consider Anabaptist Martyr a Hero." *Mennonite Weekly Review,* August 15, 1991, p. 6.

Liechty, Joseph. "Meditation on Dirk Willems." *Mennonite Life,* September 1990, pp. 18-23.

Van Braght, Thieleman J. *The Bloody Theatre, or Martyrs Mirror.* Trans. Joseph F. Sohm. Scottdale, Penn.: Herald Press, 2001.

Dirk Willems website: www.mbhistory.org/profiles/dirk.en.html.

CANTERBURY AND THE PILGRIMS' WAY, ENGLAND
by J. Nelson Kraybill

Across southern England a prehistoric footpath stretches 120 miles from Winchester to Canterbury. Predating Christianity, the road became a pilgrimage artery after Archbishop Thomas Becket was murdered in the Cathedral in 1170. He had challenged the king's authority. Pilgrims from all of Europe streamed there, some professing to experience miracles at Becket's tomb. Chaucer's *Canterbury Tales* immortalized one such pilgrimage.

The Pilgrims' Way was the principal medieval route across southern England to Canterbury. Many resources now call the footpath the North Downs Way. Coinciding with most of the route, it provides rural alternatives when the Pilgrims' Way goes through developed zones. Because the first leg from Winchester is through an urban area, you may want to start at Farnham. Canterbury is a wonderful destination: a medieval walled city with a glorious cathedral that remains the world center of Anglicanism.

Resources

Curtin, John. *North Downs Way: Farnham to Dover*. Hindhead, U.K.: Trailblazer Publications, 2006.

Curtis, Neil, and Jim Walker. *North Downs Way*. Eastbourne, U.K.: Gardners Books, 2005.

George, Christian. *Sacred Travels: Recovering the Ancient Practice of Pilgrimage*. Downers Grove, Ill.: InterVarsity Press, 2006.

Kraybill, J. Nelson. *On the Pilgrims' Way: Conversations on Christian Discipleship During a Twelve-Day Walk Across England*. Scottdale, Penn.: Herald Press, 1999.

Rambler's Association website: www.ramblers.org.uk./info/paths/northdowns.html.

COVENTRY, ENGLAND
by Eleanor Kreider

Take your family, all ages, on a day's pilgrimage to Coventry Cathedral. First you enter the ruins of the medieval Cathedral, bombed by Nazis in 1940. Pause to pray at an altar roofed by the sky. Jesus' words, "Father, forgive," are etched on the ravaged wall behind a large cross roughly shaped out of charred roof timbers. To your left looms the magnificent new cathedral, dedicated in 1962. Entering through an enormous wall of glass etched with angels and saints, you will be stunned by *Christ in Glory,* Graham Sutherland's tapestry which dominates the entire east end of the building. To your right the full-length baptistery window radiates brilliant colors, and to your left the circular Chapel of Unity beckons. The devastation of the ruins contrasts with the glory of the new cathedral, like death with resurrection.

Reconciliation is the focus of the worship and mission of the cathedral, and this pulse of Christian faith pervades everything you hear and see. Music, visual arts, liturgical conferences and educational programs—all point to the work of reconciliation and the hope of resurrection. Throughout the building are places for quiet reflection or prayer, each with a focus on a striking work of art.

Resources
Spence, Basil, and Henk Snoek. *Out of the Ashes.* London: Bles, 1963.
Coventry Cathedral website: www.coventrycathedral.org.uk.

CROAGH PATRICK, COUNTY MAYO, IRELAND
by Erin Boers
For thousands of years Croagh Patrick has been a spiritual destination for both Christians and non-Christians. Patrick, Ireland's national saint, fasted and prayed on this mountain for forty days and nights in A.D. 441. He did not come down until he had made a pact with God that granted special privileges to the Irish. More than 100,000 pilgrims now climb to the summit throughout the year. On the last Sunday in July, Reek Sunday, thousands of people make this pilgrimage on the same day.

Some proceed barefoot, some on their knees, but most prefer walking shoes and hiking sticks. The climb takes at least two hours, and the terrain is rough. Near the top, the ground becomes a steep rocky slope, where pilgrims spend nearly as much time sliding back as stepping forward. On the ascent you can confess sins to God and offer thanksgiving while experiencing breathtaking scenery. In a small chapel at the summit, mass is regularly celebrated and pilgrims can take shelter from wind or rain.

Resources

Boers, Arthur Paul. "A Pilgrimage Parable: Lessons from a Pilgrim Hike in Ireland." *The Mennonite*, March 20, 2001, pp. 4-5.

Brownlow, Tim. *Climbing Croagh Patrick.* Lantzville, B.C.: Oolichan Books, 1998.

Dublin Diocesan Jubilee Committee. *A Pilgrim's Handbook.* Dublin, Ireland: Columbia Press, 1999.

Croagh Patrick website: www.croagh-patrick.com.

GLENDALOUGH, COUNTY WICKLOW, IRELAND
by Marlene Kropf

Since the sixth century, pilgrims traveled to Glendalough, a monastic site founded by St. Kevin (b. 498) in a wooded green valley. Eventually seven churches were established in the area. The monastery was famous as a center of learning, attracting students from all over Europe. Located in a glen, the extensive ruins include stone churches, crosses with Celtic designs and one of the best-preserved round towers in Ireland.

Nearby is the cave cell that contains St. Kevin's bed made of rock. Like many early saints, Kevin was a hermit and enjoyed the company of animals. One Lent a blackbird landed on his hand and laid an egg there while Kevin was praying. He remained in prayer until the egg hatched—an example of devotion to God and God's creatures.

The visitor center introduces the area's history, archaeology and wildlife. Guided tours are available, as well as maps. What attracts Christians are the history, architecture and spectacular scenery. This is a tranquil setting for retreat and walking.

Resources

Bradley, Ian. *Celtic Christian Communities: Live the Tradition.* Kelowna, B.C.: Northstone, 2001.

Joyce, Timothy. *Celtic Christianity: A Sacred Tradition, A Vision of Hope.* Maryknoll, N.Y.: Orbis Books, 1998.

Rodgers, Michael, and Marcus Losack. *Glendalough: A Celtic Pilgrimage.* Wilton, Conn.: Morehouse Publishing, 1997.

Wicklow County website: www.wicklow.com/glendalough.

Holy Island, Lindisfarne, England

by Ray Simpson

This tidal island is known as the Cradle of Christianity to English-speaking people. In the seventh century the Irish apostle Aidan came here from Iona to bring Christian faith to pagan Anglo-Saxons. Here, he modeled "a colony of heaven," which included the first recorded school for English boys. Cuthbert, Aidan's English successor, was so influential that Alcuin, adviser to Emperor Charlemagne, declared Lindisfarne the holiest place in England.

Lindisfarne is experiencing revival as a center for pilgrims. They walk the two and a half miles across the sands between the mainland and the island, pray on St. Cuthbert's Isle, which is accessible for three hours at low tide, interact with digital presentations of the Lindisfarne Gospels and island life at the Lindisfarne Centre, linger in the Lindisfarne Gospels Garden, and explore the Priory Museum and the ruins of a later priory.

The director of St. Cuthbert's Visitors Centre leads Friday prayer walks. St. Mary's Anglican Church, built partly on the site of Aidan's original wooden church, has three daily services. The Community of Aidan and Hilda has a small retreat house, The Open Gate, and facilitates groups who want to be on the holistic edge of Christ's mission.

Resources

Simpson, Ray. *A Holy Island Prayer Book: Morning, Midday and Evening Prayer.* Norwich, U.K.: Canterbury Press, 2002; Harrisburg, Penn.: Morehouse, 2007.

Lindisfarne Island website: www.lindisfarne.org.uk.

Aidan and Hilda Community website: www.aidan.org.uk.

IONA COMMUNITY, SCOTLAND

by Willard Roth

"Behold Iona! A blessing on each eye that see-eth it." Those were Columba's words when he and a dozen disciples arrived in A.D. 563 from Ireland. From this tiny island, missionaries moved east, extending Christian faith across Scotland, England and into Europe. Pursued by Viking raiders in the eighth and ninth centuries, the monks fled Iona, likely escaping with the Book of Kells. On their return they put up high stone Celtic crosses. Samuel Johnson said, "That [person] is little to be envied . . . whose piety would not grow warmer among the ruins of Iona."

Community founder, George MacLeod, called Iona "a thin place poised between heaven and earth." Founded in the Depression, the community's original task of rebuilding ancient monastic ruins was a sign of hope for Scotland and beyond. Members bring together work and worship, prayer and politics, sacred and secular. Several months a year, pilgrims can attend week-long programs on Iona or the neighboring isle of Mull.

Resources

Boers, Arthur Paul. *The Rhythm of God's Grace.* Orleans, Mass.: Paraclete, 2003.

George, Christian. *Sacred Travels: Recovering the Ancient Practice of Pilgrimage.* Downers Grove, Ill.: InterVarsity Press, 2006.

Galloway, Kathy. *The Iona Community and Sermon in Stone.* DVD. Santa Cruz, Calif.: Wild Goose, 2006.

Millar, Peter W. *Iona.* Norwich, U.K.: Canterbury Press, 1997.

Ritchie, Anna. *Iona: The Story of an Island That Was Chosen by a Saint.* London: Batsford, 1997.

Iona Community website: www.iona.org.uk.

ISRAEL/PALESTINE

by Glenn Edward Witmer

Christianity's birthplace holds unique significance for understanding the Bible. Through the ages and from around the globe pilgrims flooded the region, some pious, others curious. Retired pastors regularly comment, "Why didn't I come years ago, when I could still make use of it in my teaching!"

Jesus drew heavily on his own surroundings for parables and stories when talking of the kingdom; it is vital we do the same to encounter new insights. At the fifth-century Council of Chalcedon, participants spoke of Jesus as "fully human and fully divine." This challenges us to better understand his human and earthly setting— a baby born under Roman occupation, living in an unheralded village, rejected by family and community, upholding Jewish beliefs yet preaching passionately against restrictiveness, confronting political and spiritual powers. "I read the Bible now in ways I never did before. The tour changed my life!"

Resources

Feiler, Bruce. *Walking the Bible: A Journey by Land through the Five Books of Moses.* New York: HarperCollins, 2002.

Pixner, Bargil. *With Jesus Through Galilee According to the Fifth Gospel.* Rosh Pina, Israel: Corazin Publishing, 1992.

First-century Nazareth village website: www.nazarethvillage.com.

JULIAN CELL, NORWICH, ENGLAND
by Marlene Kropf

Julian of Norwich (1342-1429) lived in solitude in a small room attached to the Church of St. Julian. She participated in the church's daily prayer through a window looking into the sanctuary. Another window opened to the public, providing opportunity for visitors to seek counsel from her. During a severe illness, at age 30, Julian received a series of visions of the crucified Christ. She became profoundly aware of the depth of God's eternal and all-embracing love for us. Although her era was characterized by devastating political violence and outbreaks of deadly plague, she steadfastly affirmed her faith in God's goodness: "All shall be well, and all manner of things shall be well." Thomas Merton asserted that Julian of Norwich "is the greatest of the English mystics" as well as one of the most significant English theologians.

Though the original cell was destroyed in the Reformation and the church was bombed in World War II, both have been rebuilt. Pilgrims come to visit the shrine, pray in Julian's cell and join the daily prayer of the community that meets in the church. Next door, Anglican sisters offer hospitality at All Hallows Guest House.

Resources

Colledge, Edmund, and James Walsh, trans. *Julian of Norwich: Showings.* Mahwah, N.J.: Paulist, 1978.

Jantzen, Grace M. *Julian of Norwich: Mystic and Theologian.* Mahwah, N.J.: Paulist Press, 1988.

Upjohn, Sheila. *Why Julian Now? A Voyage of Discovery.* Grand Rapids: Eerdmans, 1997.

MEDJUGORJE

by Ray Simpson

Medjugorje is a Catholic parish of 2,500 comprising two villages in Bosnia-Herzegovina. One large neighborhood church is served by Franciscans who have been open to charismatic renewal. It has become a worldwide pilgrim center, following visions given to five ordinary, "unchurchy" young people. Most of the local population responded wholeheartedly to the simple gospel messages urging them to pray always, seek reconciliation of longstanding feuds and love others. Some believe God chose this parish to be a lasting visible sign for our time, which is hungry for God's peace. This is striking, as these churches are in the crucible of deep, longstanding ethnic and ecclesiastical conflicts.

While many of the messages seem to come from Jesus' mother (a few from the risen Christ), they are based on Scripture and have borne gospel fruit. The late Pentecostal leader David du Plessis wrote: "The whole place is charged with the love of God. . . . I saw young people reading the Bible. . . . The love, unity and fellowship I saw there are only possible in the power of the Holy Spirit." There are daily church services.

Resources

Tutto, George. *Medjugorje: Our Lady's Parish.* East Sussex, U.K.: Medjugorje Information Service, 1985.

Medjugorje website: www.medjugorje.org.
Videos from Medjugorje: www.MedjugorjeVideo.com.

ROME

by Alan Kreider

Rome is, after Jerusalem, the Christian pilgrimage location par excellence. For Roman Catholics it is the site of the mother church, St. Peter's Basilica in the Vatican City. But it has many exquisite and ancient Christian places to attract pilgrims of various traditions. We consider two.

From the earliest years after Jesus' resurrection—before the arrival of Paul and Peter—there was a Christian community in Rome. Pilgrims today can visit the church of Santa Maria in Trastevere, which is a jewel, built in the Middle Ages on the site of a pre-Constantinian house church. Entering it a person is struck by its well-lit mosaics, but also by the sense that it is a place of prayer. Every evening at 8:30, hundreds of members of the Community of Sant'Egidio gather for a service of rapt worship. Afterward, members scatter across Rome to assist the city's poor—serving meals to homeless people at table, visiting them on the street and railway stations, providing showers and legal advice. This community originated in 1968 when a group of Catholic youth decided to apply the teachings of Jesus to their lives and city. It has come to have over fifty thousand members throughout Europe and around the world; it is active in international peacemaking, and in 1992 brokered the negotiations that ended the civil war in Mozambique. Visiting Trastevere today, one can worship God in the company of Christians who in many ways live the life of the early church.

Pilgrims to Rome should also visit a catacomb. Popular legend wrongly associates catacombs with secretive worship during persecution. They were, rather, underground cemeteries that expressed Christian hope, justice and compassion. Of Rome's sixty catacombs, five are open to visitors. I especially enjoy the Catacomb of Priscilla on the Via Salaria, which is entered through a convent of Benedictine sisters. The guides lead the pilgrim down into a warren of passageways lined with *loculi* (shelves) on which Christians were buried. These tunnels are punctuated by rooms in which there are frescos, the earliest Christian art form. One unforgettable room's vault is covered with paintings. At the center there is Jesus, the good Shepherd, around whom revolve depictions of motifs that embody hope: Jonah being regurgitated by the whale, a woman standing in the posture of prayer, phoenixes symbolizing everlasting life, the three persecuted young men of Daniel praying in the fiery furnace. The catacomb of Priscilla enables the pilgrim to experience the vibrancy of a church that was not afraid of death.

Resources

George, Christian. *Sacred Travels: Recovering the Ancient Practice of Pilgrimage.* Downers Grove, Ill.: InterVarsity Press, 2006.

Hager, June. *Pilgrimage: A Chronicle of Christianity Through the Churches of Rome.* London: Cassell Paperbacks, 2001.

Visser, Margaret. *The Geometry of Love: Space, Time, Mystery, and Meaning in an Ordinary Church.* Toronto: HarperFlamingoCanada, 2000.

Sant'Egidio Community website: www.santegidio.org; e-mail: info@santegidio.org.

Catacomb of Priscilla: web.tiscali.it/catacombe_priscilla; e-mail: info.priscilla@flashnet.it.

SYRIA

by Roy Hange

Pilgrimage to Syria takes one to the site of the conversion of the apostle Paul, to ancient yet active monasteries and to many Eastern Church traditions still worshiping and headquartered in Syria. Eastern Christians preserve forms of ancient prayer and rituals that draw Protestants to rediscover early roots of Christian spirituality.

A journey could move from outside the old city of Damascus at St. Paul's Convent, the place of Paul's conversion, to Ananias's house in the Christian Quarter, then down the "street called Straight," where many churches and patriarchates are located. Active monasteries and convents in the country include St. Ephrem Syrian Orthodox, St. Moses the Ethiopian, St. George's and others. Many cities have important Christian populations and beautiful churches.

Significant sites include the ruins around the Basilica of St. Simeon the Stylite in northwest Syria. (Simeon was famous for living and preaching from atop a pillar for many years.) One special experience would be to visit the country during Holy Week, when most churches have daily services with elaborate liturgical traditions.

Resources

Dalrymple, William. *From the Holy Mountain: A Journey in the Shadow of Byzantium*. London: Flamingo, 1997.

Brock, Sebastian, ed. *The Syriac Fathers on Prayer and the Spiritual Life*. Kalamazoo, Mich.: Cistercian Publications, 1987.

TAIZÉ, FRANCE

by Alissa Bender

In 1940, near the division between free and occupied France, Brother Roger founded a community with two aims: to live in communion with God through prayer and to be a leaven of peace and trust in the world. Thousands of pilgrims come annually, speaking countless languages, to join a rhythm of life shaped by prayer and song, strengthened by common work and fellowship, and seasoned by reflection and discussion.

Taizé is a witness to ecumenical harmony, with over one hundred brothers, Catholics and Protestants, representing more than twenty-five countries. Since the 1960s young people from across Europe and the globe flocked here to pray and wrestle with faith and life, while receiving hospitality. Older visitors also find a place. Bible studies, discussion groups and meal fellowship are integral parts of each day. As the entire body gathers in the Church of Reconciliation for communal prayer three times daily, the contemplative song that characterizes the community speaks at a level deeper than words.

Resources

Boers, Arthur Paul. *The Rhythm of God's Grace*. Brewster, Mass.: Paraclete, 2003.

Carey, George. *Spiritual Journey: 1000 Young Adults Share the Reconciling Experience of Taizé with the Archbishop of Canterbury*. New York: Morehouse, 1994.

George, Christian. *Sacred Travels: Recovering the Ancient Practice of Pilgrimage*. Downers Grove, Ill.: InterVarsity Press, 2006.

Spink, Kathryn. *A Universal Heart: The Life and Vision of Brother Roger of Taizé*. London: SPCK, 2005.

Taizé website: www.taize.fr.

Appendix 4

CAMINO PILGRIMAGE RESOURCES

The Camino de Santiago was one of the most important medieval pilgrimage routes. Walking these paths, the pilgrim follows the steps of such luminaries as Francis of Assisi, Dante Alighieri and Brigid of Sweden. It is emerging once more into popular consciousness. It is already well known in Europe; North Americans are becoming more aware of it too.

Several novels in the medieval mystery genre deal with the Camino: Sharan Newman's Catherine LeVendeur goes on the pilgrimage with her husband in *Strong as Death* (1996). Peter Tremayne's Celtic Sister Fidelma sets out for Santiago in *Act of Mercy* (1999). And Michael Jecks's Baldwin Furnshill and Simon Puttock make the journey in *The Templar's Penance* (2003).

Two famous non-Christian books helped sponsor New Age and heterodox fascination with the Camino: Shirley MacLaine's *The Camino: A Journey of the Spirit* (2000) and Paul Coelho's *The Pilgrimage* (1992).

Most useful in preparing a Camino pilgrimage are guidebooks, informational volumes, travelogues and websites. Several are named and described in each category below.

GUIDEBOOKS

Davies, Bethan, and Ben Cole. *Walking the Camino de Santiago.* 2nd ed.
Vancouver: Pila Pala Press, 2006. You can plan everything about

your trip with this volume, and it is light enough to carry in your pack. It deals with quirky questions, such as, Where can I fly to get near the Camino? and, What public transit is there at the start and end? It includes guides to flora and fauna, key Spanish terms and so forth. Some of the best and most memorable food I found and ate was because of recommendations here. Furthermore, this book helps one know what elevations to anticipate, always crucial in planning a day's travel.

Lozano, Millán Bravo. *A Practical Guide for Pilgrims: The Road to Santiago.* 8th ed. Translated by Sara Keane. Madrid: Editorial Everest, 2002. This lovely volume includes carefully detailed routes and gives information about *refugios*, other accommodations, food and water, restaurants, landmarks and decisions, and turns along the way. There are also small city maps and notes about historical, cultural or religious matters or sites of interest. It is too heavy to carry in one's pack, but it serves well for planning and as a keepsake afterward, with its lovely photos. It also provides separate and useful maps that are easy to carry on the pilgrimage.

Bisset, William. *The Camino Francés (St. Jean-Pied-de-Port to Santiago de Compostela).* London: Confraternity of St. James, 2007. This is justifiably one of the most popular guidebooks. It is lightweight, easy to carry, economically priced and full of practical and useful material. This volume clearly delineates distances, routes and accommodations. It is updated regularly.

INFORMATIONAL VOLUMES

Frey, Nancy Louise. *Pilgrim Stories: On and Off the Road to Santiago.* Berkeley: University of California Press, 1998. Nancy Frey is an anthropologist who has traveled the Camino more than once, served as a voluntary *hospitalero* there and encountered numerous pilgrims. She studies the Camino as a participant-observer with both affection and objectivity. Read this book ahead of time and you will be amply rewarded.

Gitlitz, David M., and Linda Kay Davidson. *The Pilgrimage Road to Santiago: The Complete Cultural Handbook*. New York: St. Martin's Griffin, 2000. This reference is a must for preparation. It has careful details about every aspect of the journey: architecture, history, folklore, saints' lives, flora and fauna. It is massive and detailed. Alas, weighing in at over four hundred pages, it is much too heavy to carry. Study it beforehand, take notes and possibly photocopy and bring sections about places you don't want to miss. (I, for example, carried a copy of the chapter on the city of Santiago and its cathedral.)

TRAVELOGUES

Hitt, Jack. *Off the Road: A Modern-Day Walk Down the Pilgrim's Route into Spain*. New York: Simon & Schuster, 1994. This articulate American writer pens a humorous account of his walk, in a style reminiscent of Bill Bryson. He writes from a secular perspective.

Hoinacki, Lee. *El Camino: Walking to Santiago de Compostela*. University Park: Penn State Press, 1996. This is an extended narrative of the author's journey at age sixty-five, before the Camino became so well known. Hoinacki is a farmer in Germany, friend of Ivan Illich, admirer of Jacques Ellul and former priest. In this stellar writing he reflects on how the Camino pushes him to consider his own life and to weigh the countercultural implications of such a journey. He discerningly critiques technology, media, television, Christian militarism and materialism. This is the best book on the Camino. Not only did it help me prepare my spirit, it offered numerous practical tips: what to carry, how to stay organized along the way, sights to see, avoiding misplacing items in *refugios*, suggested daily routines.

Rudolph, Conrad. *Pilgrimage to the End of the World: The Road to Santiago de Compostela*. Chicago: University of Chicago Press, 2004. This medieval art historian reflects on the pilgrimage as it was practiced in the Middle Ages and on his own experience of it. It includes practical tips and a number of black-and-white photos. Faith commitment is not in the forefront of this book.

Rupp, Joyce. *Walk Gently as You Go: Life Lessons from the Camino*. Maryknoll, N.Y.: Orbis, 2005. Rupp, a nun, is a justifiably popular writer on spiritual and devotional matters. She undertook this arduous journey at age sixty with an even older friend, a retired priest. This book extensively explores her learnings, especially the counsel to take life more slowly. It includes resources and practical tips.

WEBSITES

www.americanpilgrims.com. American Pilgrims on the Camino publishes a pilgrimage magazine and provides various Camino resources. They even explain where to borrow books about the Camino.

www.archicompostela.org. The Cathedral of Santiago's helpful webpage includes information about the certificate of completion and ways to prepare for the journey.

www.csj.org.uk. The Confraternity of St. James is the best English Camino resource. Through their website you can obtain books, maps, pilgrim's credential, answers to frequent questions. You can also learn what's new on the route and get in on listserve discussion forums.

www.santiago.ca. The Canadian Company of Pilgrims (formerly the Little Company of Pilgrims Canada) produces a user-friendly website full of information, opportunities to meet other pilgrims, counsel for getting ready and worship blessing resources. They too make available a pilgrim's credential.

www.santiago-compostela.net. This helpful site is provided by Spanish tourist agencies. It gives links to everything a pilgrim could want to know, including packing lists, dealing with blisters, considering weather, statistics and the like.

NOTES

Introduction

p. 19   Graceland statistics: Ken Sehested, "We Shall All Be Received in Graceland," *The Witness*, 82, nos. 7-8 (1999): 20.

p. 19   Orlando statistic: T. D. Allman, "The Theme-Parking, Megachurching, Franchising, Exurbing, McMansioning of America: How Walt Disney Changed Everything," *National Geographic*, March, 2007, p. 98.

p. 19   "set aside their lives to walk halfway across Europe": Cees Nooteboom, *Roads to Santiago: Detours and Riddles in the Lands and History of Spain*, trans. Ina Rilke (New York: Harcourt Brace, 1992), p. 50.

p. 21   Luke 9:56 is a variant reading cited in the footnote in the NRSV.

p. 23   Pilgrimage "unites belief with action": Rebecca Solnit, *Wanderlust: A History of Walking* (New York: Penguin Books, 2000), p. 50.

p. 25   "all the way to heaven is heaven": Catherine of Siena, quoted in Dorothy Day, *Selected Writings*, ed. Robert Ellsberg (Maryknoll, N.Y.: Orbis, 1992), p. 179.

p. 25   "the way is made by walking": Antonio Machado, "Proverbios y cantares XXIX," in *Campos de Castilla* (1912).

Chapter 1. I Want to Be in That Number

p. 31   "Sainthood is perhaps the only honor": Margaret Visser, *The Geometry of Love: Space, Time, Mystery, and Meaning in an Ordinary Church* (Toronto: Harper Flamingo Canada, 2000), p. 88.

p. 32   *Saunter*, from the French, *Saint Terre* or "Holy Land": Henry David Thoreau, *Walking* (San Francisco: HarperSanFrancisco, 1994), p. 2. *Saunter* might also have loaded connotations of someone who is sanctimonious, pretending to be saintly. See John Ayto, *Dictionary of Word Origins* (New York: Little, Brown, 1990), p. 458.

p. 32   Twenty religious sojourners lost half of their members: Nora Gallagher, *Things Seen and Unseen: A Year Lived in Faith* (New York: Vintage, 1998), p. 177. For further description of hardships facing medieval travelers see Jean Verdon, *Travel in the Middle Ages*, trans. George Holoch (Notre Dame, Ind.: University of Notre Dame Press, 2003).

p. 32   High cost of pilgrims' long absences: Victor Turner and Edith Turner, *Image and Pilgrimage in Christian Culture: Anthropological Perspectives* (New York: Columbia University Press, 1978), p. 38.

p. 33   "stripped the holiness from travel": Scott Russell Sanders, *Writing from the Center* (Bloomington, Ind.: Indiana University Press, 1995), p. 118.

Chapter 2. Seeking God's Homeland

p. 39   "you made us for yourself": Augustine, *Confessions*, trans. R. S. Pine-Coffin (New York: Penguin Books, 1961), p. 21.

p. 39   Bruce Chatwin quote: Bruce Chatwin, *The Songlines* (New York: Penguin Books, 1987), pp. 194-95.

p. 40   Lübeck Cathedral quote: Frederick J. Schumacher, ed., *For All the Saints: A Prayer Book For and By the Church*, vol. 4, year 2 (Delhi, N.Y.: The American Lutheran Publicity Bureau, 1996), p. 1014.

p. 40   Greek word for *way* is related to *exodus* and *odometer*: Howard Baker, *Soul Keeping: Ancient Paths of Spiritual Direction* (Colorado Springs: NavPress, 1998), p. 60.

p. 40   "Central discipleship motif": Ched Myers, *Binding the Strong Man* (Maryknoll, N.Y.: Orbis, 1988), p. 124.

p. 41   Paul as the "walkabout apostle": Robert Banks, *Reenvisioning Theological Education: Exploring a Missional Alternative to Current Models* (Grand Rapids: Eerdmans, 1999), pp. 138-39.

p. 41   Journeying has always been a key metaphor: Alister McGrath, "Classical and Modern Understandings of the Journey," *Conversations* 2, no. 2 (2004): 37-42.

p. 41   Pilgrimage is religiously motivated travel: Maribel Dietz, *Wandering Monks, Virgins, and Pilgrims: Ascetic Travel in the Mediterranean World, A.D. 300-800* (University Park: Pennsylvania State University Press, 2005), pp. 7, 64.

p. 42   "Travelers on the road to God's wisdom": Origen, quoted in Robert
               Ellsberg, *The Saints' Guide to Happiness* (New York: North Point Press,
               2003), p. 189.

p. 42   *Paroikia* means "sojourn": Patrick Henry Reardon, *Christ in the Psalms*
               (Ben Lomond, Calif.: Conciliar Press, 2000), p. 240.

p. 42   Ambulatory as a "place for walking": Margaret Visser, *The Geometry of
               Love: Space, Time, Mystery, and Meaning in an Ordinary Church* (Toronto:
               HarperFlamingoCanada, 2000), p. 56.

p. 43   Fierce opposition to pilgrimages: Philip Sheldrake, *Spaces for the Sacred:
               Place, Memory, and Identity* (Baltimore, Md.: Johns Hopkins University
               Press, 1994), p. 45.

p. 43   Pilgrimage as an internal journey: Jane Leach, "Camino de Santiago:
               The Value and Significance of Pilgrimage in the Twenty-first Cen-
               tury," *Epworth Review* 33, no. 1 (2006): 32.

p. 44   Christians as a "band of people 'on the move'": Visser, *Geometry of
               Love*, p. 95.

p. 44   Statistics on Christian sites in the Holy Land: Victor Turner and
               Edith Turner, *Image and Pilgrimage in Christian Culture: Anthropological Per-
               spectives* (New York: Columbia University Press, 1978), p. 38.

Chapter 3. Lord, Teach Us to Be Prayerful

p. 48   Anne Lamott's two basic prayers: Anne Lamott, *Traveling Mercies: Some
               Thoughts on Faith* (New York: Pantheon, 1999), p. 82.

p. 48   Prayer as "keeping company with God": Clement of Alexandria,
               cited in James Houston, *The Transforming Friendship: A Guide to Prayer*
               (Oxford: Lion, 1989), p. 6.

Chapter 4. Your Pack's Too Big

p. 56   "Your Feet's Too Big": Fats Waller, "Your Feet's Too Big" (1939), lyr-
               ics by Ada Benson and Fred Fisher.

p. 59   "Whether it was the apostles": Robert Ellsberg, *The Saints' Guide to
               Happiness: Everyday Wisdom from the Lives of the Saints* (New York: North
               Point Press, 2003), p. 142.

p. 64   "One of the penalties of an ecological education": Aldo Leopold,
               Round River (New York: Oxford University Press, 1993), p. 165.

Chapter 5. The Road That Leads to Life

p. 69   T. S. Eliot's pilgrim poem, "Little Gidding," *The Top 500 Poems,* ed. William Harmon (New York: Columbia University Press, 1992), pp. 987-94.

Chapter 6. The Journey Is Long

p. 77   "all comparison injures": Søren Kierkegaard, *Purity of Heart Is to Will One Thing,* trans. Douglas V. Steere (New York: Harper & Row, 1948), p. 208.

Chapter 7. Well, That's the Camino

p. 101   the culture of the table: I recommend three books by Albert Borgmann: *Crossing the Postmodern Divide* (Chicago: University of Chicago Press, 1992); *Power Failure: Christianity in the Culture of Technology* (Grand Rapids: Brazos, 2003); *Technology and the Character of Contemporary Life: A Philosophical Inquiry* (Chicago: University of Chicago Press, 1984).

p. 102   "A shared meal is the activity": Christine D. Pohl, *Making Room: Recovering Hospitality as a Christian Tradition* (Grand Rapids: Eerdmans, 1999), p. 30.

p. 106   "principalities and powers": William Stringfellow explored these ideas at length in several books. Two places, among others, where he reflected on the vocation of powers and principalities include *Free in Obedience* (New York: Seabury, 1964), pp. 52-53, and *An Ethic for Christians and Other Aliens in a Strange Land* (Waco, Tex.: Word, 1973), pp. 57-58.

Chapter 8. *No "Ustedes" por Favor*

p. 111   "Servile and ceremonial forms of speech": George Orwell, cited in Nora Gallagher, *Things Seen and Unseen: A Year Lived in Faith* (New York: Vintage Books, 1998), p. 70.

p. 114   "There is no one I'd rather be with": Albert Borgmann, from a consultation with Albert Borgmann and Eugene Peterson in Missoula, Montana, March 2001, of which I was a part.

p. 116   "Be compassionate": Philo of Alexandria, unknown source.

Chapter 9. Secular Seekers

p. 122   Medieval pilgrims, their motivations and shortcomings: Jean Verdon,

Travel in the Middle Ages, trans. George Holoch (Notre Dame, Ind.: University of Notre Dame Press, 2003), pp. 217ff. A fourth-century Galician heresy is discussed in Maribel Dietz, *Wandering Monks, Virgins, and Pilgrims: Ascetic Travel in the Mediterranean World A.D. 300-800* (University Park: Pennsylvania State University Press, 2005), p. 164.

p. 128 Six thousand pilgrimage sites: Craig Bartholomew and Robert Llewelyn, introduction to *Explorations in a Christian Theology of Pilgrimage,* ed. Craig Bartholomew and Fred Hughes (Burlington, Vt.: Ashgate, 2004), p. xii.

p. 130 "I think I should be tempted to go": John Burroughs, "The Exhilarations of the Road," in *The Magic of Walking,* eds. Aaron Sussman and Ruth Goode (New York: Simon & Schuster, 1967), p. 267.

Chapter 10. Focal Ways of Life

p. 133 The merit of "staying put": Scott Russell Sanders, *Staying Put: Making Home in a Restless World* (Boston: Beacon Press, 1993).

p. 134 "There is a restlessness within us": Sigurd F. Olson, *The Singing Wilderness* (New York: Albert A. Knopf, 1957), pp. 6-7.

pp. 134-35 "lead to a disconnected, disembodied": Ibid., p. 108.

p. 135 Focal concerns that "center and illuminate our lives": Albert Borgmann, *Technology and the Character of Contemporary Life: A Philosophical Inquiry* (Chicago: University of Chicago Press, 1984), p. 4.

p. 136 "Focal reality gathers and illuminates our world": Albert Borgmann, *Crossing the Postmodern Divide* (Chicago: University of Chicago Press, 1992), p. 96.

Chapter 11. Walking in Faith

p. 145 Americans walk just a few hundred yards a day: Bill Bryson, *A Walk in the Woods: Rediscovering America on the Appalachian Trail* (New York: Broadway Books, 1998), p.129.

p. 146 not only walking on water is a marvel: Thich Nhat Hanh, *The Long Road Turns to Joy: A Guide to Walking Meditation* (Berkeley, Calif.: Parallax Press, 1996), p. 58.

p. 146 Feet as bearers of truth: Richard D. Patterson, "The Biblical Imagery of Feet as a Vehicle for Truth," *Bibliotheca Sacra* 163 (2006): 29-45.

p. 148 *Solvitur ambulando:* often attributed to Augustine, although that cannot be confirmed. The exact source of this quote cannot be found.

p. 151   "to pay attention to the deepest thing [I] know": Douglas Steere, *To-gether in Solitude* (New York: Crossroad, 1982), p. 25.

p. 154   "It is dry and scorching hot in the summer": Nancy Louise Frey, *Pil-grim Stories: On and Off the Road to Santiago* (Berkeley: University of California Press, 1998), pp. 76-77.

Chapter 12. Here I Walk, I Can Do No Other

p. 161   "to both faster speeds and greater stimulation": Linda Breen Pierce, "Time by Design," in *Take Back Your Time: Fighting Overwork and Time Poverty in America*, ed. John de Graaf (San Francisco: Berrett-Koehler, 2003), p. 198.

p. 162   Pauses, breaks and respites: Ralph Keyes speaks about the "*pauses we've eliminated from everyday life*" in *Timelock: How Life Got So Hectic and What You Can Do About It* (New York: Harper, 1991), p. 97.

p. 162   Time can be "dead" or "live": Pierce, "Time by Design."

p. 163   "the three mile an hour God": Kosuke Koyama, *Three Mile an Hour God: Biblical Reflections* (Maryknoll, N.Y.: Orbis, 1979), p. 7.

p. 167   The Bible is an outdoor book: Wendell Berry, "Christianity and the Survival of Creation," in *Sex, Economy, Freedom & Community* (New York: Pantheon, 1992), p. 103.

p. 168   "the wonder has leaked out": Eugene H. Peterson, *Christ Plays in Ten Thousand Places* (Grand Rapids: Eerdmans, 1989), p. 57.

Conclusion

p. 177   "the best possible thing for your salvation": Meister Eckhart quotation posted on the wall of a parlor at St. Gregory's Abbey, Three Rivers, Michigan.

p. 178   "Since God is near to all who call upon him": Abbess Samantham, cited in Edward C. Sellner, *Pilgrimage* (Notre Dame, Ind.: Sorin Books, 2004), p. 158.

p. 178   "We shall not cease exploration": T. S. Eliot, "Little Gidding," *The Top 500 Poems*, ed. William Harmon (New York: Columbia University Press, 1992), pp. 987-94.

p. 178   Film John Travolta starred in: *A Love Song for Bobby Long*, directed by

Shainee Gabel (2004).

p. 178 "Pilgrims often journey to the ends of the earth": Scott Russell Sanders, *Staying Put: Making Home in a Restless World* (Boston: Beacon Press, 1993), p. 154.

Appendix I. Recovering and Reclaiming Christian Pilgrimage

p. 179 "A pilgrimage is a journey": Paul Elie, *The Life You Save May Be Your Own: An American Pilgrimage* (New York: Farrar, Straus & Giroux, 2003), p. x.

p. 179 a way of appropriating the story for oneself: from Rosemary Mahoney, *The Singular Pilgrim: Travels on Sacred Ground* (New York: Houghton Mifflin, 2003), p. 274.

p. 180 "cursed, since it was the site of the Crucifixion": Maribel Dietz, *Wandering Monks, Virgins, and Pilgrims* (University Park: Pennsylvania State University Press, 2005), p. 129.

p. 180 "Therefore let this principle abide with us": Columbanus, cited in Philip Sheldrake, *Spaces for the Sacred: Place, Memory and Identity* (Baltimore, Md.: Johns Hopkins University Press, 2001), p. 116.

p. 181 "To go to Rome means great toil and little profit": Edward C. Sellner, *Pilgrimage* (Notre Dame, Ind: Ave Maria Press, 2004), p. 93.

p. 181 "As pilgrims and strangers in this world": Francis of Assisi, in Sheldrake, *Spaces for the Sacred*, p. 117.

p. 181 Jesuits modeling "a spirituality of mission and mobility": Ibid.

p. 182 "We go on the pilgrim way": Tom Wright, *The Way of the Lord: Christian Pilgrimage Today* (Grand Rapids: Eerdmans, 1999), pp. 9-11, 130.

p. 182 Several types of Christian pilgrimages: E. Alan Morinis, introduction to *Sacred Journeys* (Westport, Conn.: Greenwood, 1992), pp. 10-13, quoted in Nancy Louise Frey, *Pilgrim Stories: On and Off the Road to Santiago* (Berkeley: University of California Press, 1998), p. 262.
         A highly recommended resource is Craig Bartholomew and Fred Hughes, eds., *Explorations in a Christian Theology of Pilgrimage* (Burlington, Vt.: Ashgate, 2004). The editors address an unfortunate gap in systematic theological reflection on pilgrimage. The volume has essays on such topics as "Pilgrimage and 'Place': an Old Testament View," "Pilgrimage and the New Testament," "Paul and Pilgrimage," "Pilgrimage in the Early Church," "Protestants and Pilgrimage." Espe-

cially helpful are reflections on the Holy Land and issues associated with pilgrimages there. This volume is particularly sensitive to evangelical themes and concerns.

p. 182   "The prostitution of foreign and exotic places": Lee Hoinacki, *El Camino: Walking to Santiago de Compostela* (University Park: Pennsylvania State University Press, 1996), p. 247.

p. 183   Something called "spiritual tourism": Adrian J. Ivakhiv, *On Sacred Ground: Pilgrims and Politics at Glastonbury and Sedona* (Bloomington: Indiana University Press, 2001), p. xi.

p. 183   "goal-centered, religious travel": Dietz, *Wandering Monks, Virgins, and Pilgrims*, p. 7.

p. 184   "The pilgrim slows down, moves in God's time": William Fitzgerald, "The Blessings of Pilgrimage," *Praying* 86 (1998): 16.

p. 184   "The Camino is a process": Barbara Haab, "The Way as an Inward Journey: An Anthropological Enquiry into the Spirituality of Present-day Pilgrims to Santiago, Part 1," trans. Howard Nelson, *Confraternity of Saint James Bulletin*, May 1996, p. 29.

Appendix 2. Planning a Christian Pilgrimage

p. 189   Reentry culture shock: Nancy Louise Frey, "Pilgrimage and Its Aftermaths," in *Intersecting Journeys: The Anthropology of Pilgrimage and Tourism*, ed. Ellen Badone and Sharon R. Roseman (Urbana: University of Illinois Press, 2004), p. 99.

p. 191   We do not do well at integrating pilgrimage learning: Barbara Haab, "The Way as an Inward Journey: An Anthropological Enquiry into the Spirituality of Present-day Pilgrims to Santiago, Part 2," trans. Howard Nelson *Confraternity of Saint James Bulletin*, May 1996, p. 34.

Appendix 3. Pilgrimage Destinations

p. 192   "historical enquiry bathed in prayer": Peter Walker, "Pilgrimage in the Early Church," in *Explorations in a Christian Theology of Pilgrimage*, ed. Craig Bartholomew and Fred Hughes (Burlington, Vt.: Ashgate, 2004), p. 88.

p. 198   "Behold Iona!": Presbuteros (Anonymous), "Iona," *The Expository Times*, August 1988, p. 352.

p. 198   "That [person] is little to be envied": Quoted in John Marsden, *The*

Illustrated Life of Columba, trans. John Gregory (Edinburgh: Floris Books, 1995), p. 232.

p. 198 "a thin place poised between heaven and earth": Quoted in Robert K. Gustafson, "Iona Expands," *The Christian Century,* January 15 1986, pp. 48-49.

p. 200 "All shall be well": Julian of Norwich, *Julian of Norwich: Showings,* trans. Edmund Colledge and James Walsh (New York: Paulist Press, 1978), p. 305.

p. 200 Julian, greatest of the English mystics: Thomas Merton, *Mystics and Zen Masters* (New York: Delta, 1967), p. 140.

p. 201 "The whole place is charged with the love of God": David du Plessis, quoted in George Tutto, *Medjugorje: Our Lady's Parish* (East Sussex, U.K.: Medjugorje Information Service, 1985), p. 21.